The Essential Lymphatic Health Handbook

Sumaiyah .M Weber

All rights reserved.

Copyright © 2024 Sumaiyah .M Weber

The Essential Lymphatic Health Handbook : Unlock Your Body's Healing Potential with the Complete Guide to Lymphatic Health

<u>Funny helpful tips:</u>

Regularly reassess business goals; evolving them as the market changes.

Incorporate lean proteins; they support muscle growth and provide sustained energy.

Life advices:

Stay authentic; genuine interactions build trust and rapport.

Prioritize a balanced diet; the nutrients you consume play a pivotal role in determining your overall health and energy levels.

Introduction

The lymphatic system plays a vital role in our overall health and well-being. Understanding its functions and learning how to boost lymph flow can greatly improve our health and make us feel great. This guide aims to provide valuable insights into the lymphatic system and offer practical tips to optimize its function.

The lymphatic system is a complex network of vessels, nodes, and organs responsible for removing toxins, waste, and excess fluids from our body tissues. It plays a crucial role in supporting the immune system and maintaining a healthy balance in the body.

However, in today's fast-paced world, our lymphatic system faces challenges due to increased stress and inadequate rest. These factors can lead to sluggish lymph flow, which manifests through various signs like swelling, fatigue, and frequent illnesses.

To support the lymphatic system, it is essential to stay hydrated and consume fresh, organic, and unprocessed foods. Ensuring a more alkaline diet can also help maintain a healthy lymph flow.

Incorporating green foods and hydrating fruits into our diet can further enhance lymph function. Juicing is an excellent way to boost nutrient intake and support lymph health.

Enzymes, herbs, and spices can be beneficial for improving lymphatic flow. Including these nutrients in our diet can aid in detoxification and support overall lymph health.

Exercise and movement play a vital role in boosting lymph flow. Self-help lymphatic moves, such as walking, bouncing, and stretching, can effectively stimulate lymphatic circulation.

Yoga, especially lymphatic yoga, can also be highly beneficial. Pranayama and mudras are valuable practices that support lymph flow and promote overall well-being.

Incorporating self-help massage techniques, like dry skin brushing, can further stimulate lymphatic circulation and help eliminate toxins from the body.

Sweating and staying hydrated are essential for supporting the lymphatic system. Engaging in activities that bring joy and laughter can also positively impact lymphatic flow.

Understanding the connection between our heart and lymphatic system can guide us in finding stress relief and achieving a state of balance.

Making lifestyle changes, like reducing stress and practicing healthy habits, can significantly improve lymph function and overall health.

By avoiding factors that hinder lymph system function, such as tight clothing and toxic beauty products, we can promote a healthier lymphatic system.

In conclusion, optimizing lymph flow is essential for maintaining overall health and vitality. By following the tips and practices outlined in this guide, individuals can support their lymphatic system and experience the benefits of a well-functioning immune system and improved well-being. Remember that small changes in daily habits and incorporating self-help practices can make a significant difference in our lymphatic health and overall quality of life.

Contents

About the Lymphatic System 1
What Is the Lymphatic System? 2
Increasing Stress and Less Rest 10
Toxins, Hydration and the Lymph 14
Signs of Sluggish Lymph 16
Stay Hydrated 21
Less Acid More Alkaline 27
The Inner Terrain, Still a New Frontier 32
Eat Fresh, Organic, Unprocessed Foods 36
Get Your Green 39
Drink your Meal 41
Food Experimenting Can Be Good For Your Health 43
Hydrating Food 45
Take a Step 50
Seeing Red in a Good Way 50
To Health, Those Colorful Flavonoids 52
Juicing for Vitality 55
Improving Lymph Function with Enzymes, Herbs, Spices and Other Nutrients 59
    Enzymes 59
    Herbs and Spices 61
An Ounce of Prevention is Worth a Pound of Cure 69
Self-Help Good Lymph Moves 71
Self-Help Walking 72
Self-Help Get a Jump on It! 73

Bouncing While Standing..74
    Jumping for Joy 75
Self-Help Lymph Stretches 75
    1.   Neck Roll Side-to-Side 76
    2.   Head Tilt 76
    3.   Shoulder Roll 76
    4.   Shoulder Shrug 77
    5.   Elbow Bend 77
    6.   Pelvic Tilt 77
    7.   Leg Flexing 77
    8.   Ankle Pumps 78
Self-Help Stomach Crunches 78
Full Breathing...78
The Breath and Stress...79
Self-Help Learning to Breathe Again...81
Self-Help Horizontal Health Squat...82
Yoga...84
    Lymphatic Yoga 85
    Pranayama 85
    Mudras 86
Self-Help Breath and Mudras 86
Self-Help Diaphragmatic Breathing 86
    Self-help Mudras for the Lymph 87
Self-Help Thoracic Drainage 89
Self-Help Lymph in the Upper Body 90
Self-Help at the Digestive Center 90
Self-Help Lymph Reflexes on the Feet 93

Self-Help Windshield Wipers (aka, ScissorKicks) 93
Self-Help Dailies 94
    Acupressure discs 94
    Stand tall 94
    Chair poses 95
Self-Help Massage and Aromatherapy 96
Self-Help Dry Skin Brushing 99
Self-Help Sweating 103
Self-Help Water Cures 103
Feeling Fully Alive 109
Laughter and Joy 111
Get Happy 112
Heart Waves 115
Finding Stress Relief in Head-Heart Balance 116
The Heart as GPS 119
The Water That Flows 123
Top Take-Aways to Optimize Lymph Function 125
Toward Greater Lymph Flow 125
Some of the Best Ingestibles for Lymph Function 127
Making Lifestyle Changes 131
My Favorite Take-away 132
Remember, These Are Ways We Hinder LymphSystem Function 132

[1]
About the Lymphatic System

As we develop in the womb, "we are all water babies," as the title of the book by Jessica Johnson and Michel Odent so aptly describes. We literally grow, like little tadpoles, in the inner ocean of our mother's waters of life. Not only do we grow in a watery environment, when we are born, our composition is mostly water — estimates range from 70-75%. As we age, we too often develop bad habits and addictions to things like caffeine, alcohol, sugar and highly processed foods that actually use a lot of the body's liquid resources to process, essentially stealing it from more vital functions. Instead of drinking glasses of water, we sip water like we sip beverages, when our body is actually starving for this most precious substance.

Unfortunately, it's not uncommon to hear comments from people saying that they don't like to drink water. I recently overheard someone at a cafe say, "I drink coffee like water." Well, this is a direction that needs to be course-corrected as soon as possible.

Why does this matter? Because our fluid systems are absolutely essential to our health and well-being. We need water to live, and a sufficient amount of it to thrive. When we think of our inner fluids, we usually think of the heart's circulatory system or how we move fluid through the kidneys' filtration and the elimination process through the urinary track. Throughout all the liquid-filled chambers and vessels in our body, water-based solutions act as highly effective systems of communication and transport to keep us alive and functioning. One of the best-kept secrets of our biology is the lymphatic system. It is a vital fluid system that is quite crucial to how well we feel and how healthy we are.

The lymphatic fluid is part of the inner ocean of water that we are, a very important facet of how we clean our bodies of toxins and infectious agents. The composition of the lymph is very close to that of the interstitial fluid, from which it is directly derived. As an indication of how important the lymphatic system is, its fluid is double the volume of the blood in our bodies. If this particular fluid system stopped functioning, we would have up to a few days to live —it's that crucial.

Water is the universal medium of healing and cleansing. The lymph fluid is the medium that carries substances that need to be removed in order to keep the body free of harmful contaminants and intruders, such as viruses, and opportunistic bacteria. If we do not have enough water volume in our body for all the key elements that it handles, then the lymph's role to detoxify the body is lessened. One of the ways this will be expressed is by slowing the escort of foreign agents from the body and in essence fostering sluggish and thicker, more acidic lymph fluid.

One of the most important things you can do to help your lymph system to function is to stay hydrated by drinking water in an amount that equals one-half of the body's weight in fluid ounces per day. Because most of us don't have our water palate developed these days, we slip in sugary beverages, tea, coffee and alcoholic drinks, such as wine or beer, that satisfy our mental and emotional appetites more than what our body is truly calling for.

Drinking pure water, with its natural cleansing capacity intact, will go a long way to keep the body healthy. Yet increasingly we are forgetting how well designed the body is and how it is meant to take care of us in seamless and highly intelligent ways. This book is a guide to provide lifestyle options and simple practices that can keep us feeling vital and fluid in a good way.

What Is the Lymphatic System?

The lymphatic system, usually called simply the lymph, is probably the most overlooked body system that we have. It is also quite key to our health. John Douillard, D.C., a well known Ayurvedic specialist, has written that even doctors have traditionally had little awareness of its vital importance in health. He knows this because for years he trained many of them while co-directing an Ayurvedic cancer center with Deepak Chopra. The doctors knew about removing cancer from the nodes but didn't know of the prime significance of the lymph system *before* disease arose. Fortunately, medical awareness of the role of the lymph is on the rise.

According to Dr. Douillard, in Ayurveda, the lymph—or 'rasa,' as they call it—is the primary focus for treatment of *any* condition. Evidently, Ayurveda knows how significant the lymph is. This ancient wisdom system describes the lymph as 'longevity juice.'

With all the good focus on detox in this country, it is now time for the lymph system to take center stage as we learn about how to foster better function of our 'longevity juice' system. While mostly unknown to us until now, the lymphatic system is a major invisible ally.

The lymph has been described as a liquid transportation network, a highly sophisticated surveillance system, a finely developed filtration system, a detox plant, a defense system, and a low-pressure drainage operation. Since its discovery and study in the West, it has been described more organically as an aquarium and an inner ocean. One of the first Western scientists that identified the lymph system, Thomas Bartholin from Denmark, described it well; "the lymph system is a natural cleansing and watering system." To contemporary Dr. Gerald Lemole it is 'a river of life.' Dr. Chikly has called the lymph an 'elixir of life' very much in keeping with the Ayurvedic understanding of its highly significant role.

People who know anything about the lymph usually know it as the body's waste drainage system. The lymph is designed to transport foreign agents, metabolic debris and toxins away from the cells. This is big work that it does for us to the extent it is not compromised in its ability to function. Until recently, the lymph's work was more focused on removing agents within nature that are antagonistic—foreign bodies and pathogenic agents. Today, though, the lymph has a huge challenge, being a key member of the internal team to clear manmade toxins that make it into the tissues.

The lymphatic system consists of a vast network of capillaries, vessels, nodes, ducts and lymph fluids throughout the body. This system begins with a tiny permeable network of capillaries, leading into larger lymph vessels. The lymph system manages the flow of its liquid with valves in some of its vessels, through this one-way system of channels. The vessels drain into larger passageways, the two major returns known as ducts. The lymph's major connector, the left thoracic duct, delivers fluids back to the venous part of the circulatory system right before the heart.

While most information about the lymph focuses on its detox role, it is foremost an alkaline liquid system that bathes the cells so that food nutrients and oxygen from the blood system can actually reach and feed the cells. If the ability of the lymph to clear the waste from the cells diminishes, then the delivery of vital nutrients to the cells is also lessened. Without this supply, the cells can become vulnerable and weakened, and this kind of situation increases the potential for cell mutation from the continuing stress of a toxic inner milieu—the surrounding bath of fluids.

So the lymphatic system is first and foremost a fluid system. Itself 96% water, it has a primary role to manage the body's inner fluid balance in the tissues 24/7. It does this by absorbing excess fluids that have leaked from the blood circulatory system into connective tissues. Most of the plasma that leaks is reabsorbed right back into the blood system. The portion of the blood plasma that does not becomes known as interstitial fluid, meaning fluid within the tissue spaces. Once the lymph capillaries sponge it up, then it becomes lymph fluid.

Most experts indicate that the volume of leaked fluids each day can reach 10%. One key expert, Dr. Chikly, indicates this volume can be as much as 20% of fluid leakage that the lymph system is charged with reabsorbing. In its passage through the lymph capillaries, vessels and ducts, most of this fluid is filtered through the nodes before being returned to the venous part of the circulatory system.

The lymph reabsorbs large proteins that are constantly leaking from the blood system in minute amounts. If it did not, the tissues in the body would begin swelling, a condition known as edema. The lymph fluid is so vital that it returns close to half of the body's circulating protein on a daily basis back into the blood circulatory system. Its role as transport for these proteins is so critical that if it stopped, then we would have a day or two at most to live.

Dr. Lemole, one of the most well known medical writers on this subject, has indicated that the functioning of the lymph system is involved in 70% of all chronic disease. He has suggested that by keeping the lymph clear and flowing, we could eliminate a majority of modern-day diseases. This high number suggests the need to pay attention and learn more about this little known but highly significant system. Yet the lymph system is still a mystery to most.

Much of the work of the lymphatic system is uphill, and not just because of the barrage of manmade toxins that our bodies are inundated with in the present-day world. The lymphatic system is quite literally a system of one-way channels to deliver the overflow back to the venous system in the chest, right before the heart. This system does not have a direct heart pump, as the circulatory system does, lymph primarily moves due to muscular contractions in surrounding tissues. The other major catalyst for this fluid movement occurs from breathing. Gravity also plays a role in helping the lymph through its inner system of waterways.

The lymph system has such a strong interrelationship with the body's defense system that it is characterized as helping to regulate the immune system. A compromised lymph system is not only degraded in its ability to detox; there is a direct effect of diminishing the body's immunity and vitality.

The lymph system and the immune system are interconnected to such a degree that it is no wonder then that the lymphoid organs are also the body's sites of defense. Dr. Haas characterizes the lymphatic system as "the circulatory system of your body's immune defense system," an insight so important that should we should grow up knowing it. The bone marrow is a primary site where the body's lymphocytes are produced. Some of the lymphocytes mature there and become B-cells. The thymus, located in the heart area, is the other major site for the body's agents of immune defense known as T-cells to develop.

Other lymph system organs are the tonsils, adenoids, and the spleen. The spleen is a major organ that works to filter blood and lymph fluid to keep the body free of infections. As part of the lymph system, the spleen also plays a role in maintaining inner fluid balance as well as clearing cellular debris and recycling worn-out cells, such as damaged red blood cells.

Small clusters of lymph tissue are located in areas of the body where filtration matters most. Most people don't know about the vital role that the Peyer's Patches tissue plays in surveillance, monitoring what goes through the small intestine to flag anything that may be unfriendly to issue a call for an immune response. In the large intestine the appendix helps protect against invading microorganisms. The tonsils and adenoids are likewise positioned in the upper body as defense outposts to keep foreign agents from entering the body.

A majority of the body's lymph tissue is found under our intestinal tissue lining. Some refer to this as GALT, or Gut Associated Lymph

Tissue. There is a very close relationship between how well the intestines are functioning and how well our lymph system is working overall because they are so interrelated. In the intestines, tiny hairs called villi are vital workers in helping the body take in food substances by increasing the surface area of absorption, which is especially helpful for fatty acid digestion. These tiny hairs are also involved in the movement of food substances through the intestines.

Keeping the villi intact is not only good for digestion. Lymph capillaries in the intestines called lacteals play on the same team with the villi; a single lacteal is found inside each strand of villus. The lacteals have the job to pick up and transport fatty acids to larger lymph channels. Yet when there are digestive disturbances (i.e., food allergies and sensitivities or toxic intake), it can create irritations that have a deleterious effect on the villi's ability to function. Since the two are designed to work together, if the villi are compromised, the lacteals are negatively affected as well.

Derived from blood, lymph fluid is similar, but with a higher water content than the blood, which suits its role as form of internal fluid transport. It is closest in composition to the interstitial fluid that it picks up from outside the cells. The lymph system does not transport red blood cells to any appreciable degree. Proteins and fats are two of the most important nutrients that it conveys daily. Most of the time the fluid is mostly clear. When it is transporting lipids from the intestines it can be whitish from the higher fat load. It also contains minerals, enzymes, hormones, dissolved gases such as nitrogen and carbon dioxide, and other waste since it has a role to transport these substances so the body can remove them. This waste includes infectious material from foreign agents as well as the body's own metabolic waste from its daily work.

The areas of greatest lymph concentration are the intestinal system, the neck and in the dermis of the skin. The lungs are also an area where lymph is well populated. From the small lymph capillaries, the fluid travels to larger passageways, known as vessels, with one-way valves to filtering stations known as nodes. This vast inner waterway has twice the number of vessels as the blood system.

The body has between 400-1,000 nodes, ranging from barely visible threads to the size of a small bean. The lymph fluid circulates through this extensive network of fine filters that defend the body and keep it intact and healthy. The nodes are sites where harmful substances such as viruses, opportunistic bacteria and even cancer cells are trapped and broken down for removal. Acting as sentinels of defense, the nodes also have a role to stimulate the immune system when necessary.

The nodes in the neck make up about one-third of the entire system of lymph filtration. When nodes are actively fighting an infection, they will appear swollen. When this happens in the neck area, we often say that we have 'swollen glands,' yet what we really have are enlarged lymph nodes doing their work to orchestrate the body's defense system and clear foreign bodies that need to be eliminated.

In our development, the lymph literally sprouts from the veins, so it is highly interrelated with the circulatory system. Yet the lymph is a slow-flow system of inner fluid transport without a heart pump. Indeed, John Ossipinsky, a devoted researcher and certified lymph therapist, has rightly called it the "other circulatory system." Some even indicate that the lymphatic system is part of the circulatory system. Even scientists in vascular biology and medicine are beginning to re-evaluate whether this system is secondary or primary, based on breakthroughs in research in the past decade. With it gaining new research interest, we can look forward to new revelations about the vital role of the lymphatic system. As indicated earlier, from an ancient Ayurvedic standpoint, the lymph system is primary.

The lymph is constantly working in tandem with the immune system. Dr. Lemole has described the lymphatic system as our own 'center for disease control.' The lymph fluid carries lymphocytes to wherever they are needed to maintain 'homeland security' within the interior. There are three major types of lymphocytes: T-cells, B-cells, and the NK or natural killer cells.

Another key aspect of proper internal lymph flow involves the body's internal messaging systems. One example, the proper movement of fluids is vital for timely communication from the lymph tissue to the nodes and thymus to make sure that the right type of lymphocytes are produced to resist invading organisms.

Dr. Stanley Rockson heads up the Lymphedema Clinic at the Stanford University School of Medicine. A cutting edge researcher on the lymphatic system and its disorders, Dr. Rockson provides more of an overview: the lymph system is "responsible for communication within the area around the cell, for supporting the fluid environment surrounding cells and between tissues, and also for maintaining the volume of that fluid." This is a far more encompassing role than most of us have any clue about.

According to Dr. Chikly, another way that this system is a key center is indicated by the feedback loop that happens when there is greater flow of fluid through the nodes. With increased flow, the body also ups the production of lymphocytes. He uses it to make the point that professional techniques like he has developed can be very effective in helping the body to enhance its defense mechanisms through lymphocyte production to protect and preserve. How smart is that? When describing the lymph system we focus on its role in defense and clearing, but it's role to communicate, to deliver messages in order to regulate function, is likely as key. It certainly is a much-needed subject for new avenues of research.

Along with the lymphocytes, macrophages are immune system cells that exist in every form of tissue throughout the body. These are among the most adaptive of all cells, capable of morphing to express different characteristics depending on where these little powerhouses are placed for defense. I think of the macrophage form as the original Pac Man, energetically pursuing and gobbling up substances that are deemed harmful (such as viruses and cancer cells) or no longer needed in the body (dead cells). Together with the lymphocytes, they work in the lymph nodes to destroy foreign cells. Known as the 'big eaters' of our body, they engulf bodies that are identified as foreign and basically compost them down to their basic elements to be recycled or eliminated. Our body is so intelligent, it is constantly assessing what is in the best interests for optimal health.

Increasing Stress and Less Rest

According to chiropractor and Ayurvedic expert Dr. John Douillard, "Stress has been identified as the cause of about 80% of all disease. The chemistry of stress is degenerative and lymph congesting." Dr. Elson Haas has indicated that stress makes the lymphocytes less effective in their work to protect us.

It's interesting that stress has such a major involvement in disease and that it causes the lymph to decrease its ability to keep the body clear. Cardiologist and lymph expert Dr. Lemole has stated that a clogged lymph system is involved in the development of 70% of major disease conditions such as heart disease, cancer and arthritis.

In order to maintain better health, we need to decrease stress, and increase adaptation and resilience as we become educated and actively in favor of our lymph. This book is dedicated to offer options that boost the flow of lymph and to live well.

Stress itself promotes an acidic chemistry in the body that contributes negatively to the toxic cycle that overburdens the body and can lead to degenerative disease. Living a stressful life without supportive practices and foods will quickly hinder body systems from functioning well, so it's a quick way to accelerate aging. We think of stress as being psychological, but eating foods that are harmful is itself a stress to the body, as are continuing thoughts, such as worry, that circulate without resolution. Other forms of stress include dehydration, not having an adequate level of water intake to maintain the body's vital fluid systems properly. It's a factor in raising cortisol, which reinforces the point that fluids really are crucial.

What we call stress usually means that we have become distressed, meaning an issue remains unresolved over time and the stress continues unabated. Our bodies are designed for a certain level of 'stress,' otherwise known as challenges in life. The sympathetic nervous system perceives a challenge and increases signals to become more alert and get ready for action. When we are able to move forward on an issue, we meet the challenge, and then the nervous system recognizes that it no longer has to gear up for some event. Then it switches to the parasympathetic system, our relaxing, cooling and rebuilding system.

The founder of polarity therapy, Dr. Randolph Stone, was a brilliant osteopath, chiropractor and naturopath who made many major contributions to the understanding of how the nervous system functions. He indicated that in the modern world, we are doing damage to our nervous system because we are too often 'turned on,' in sympathetic system activation mode. We are designed to be primarily in the resting and rebuilding portion of the nervous function, the parasympathetic system. Dr. Stone was writing and working up to the mid-1970s. His insights are even more relevant today.

Since the 1970s, the computer revolution has occurred, and use of the Internet has become a common phenomenon of our lives. Now, technology moves at warp speed. This constantly accelerating rate of change is having a marked effect upon our lifestyle and behavior as well. While it's great to have the access that technology makes possible and to be able to realize true advances in the world, presently we are too often missing much-needed balance. The speed of life has an effect on how well our own body systems function that too often registers with the general malaise known as 'stress.'

Much of what we call stress is an inherent part of living in a way that causes our sympathetic system to be continually turned on, using up our inner physical resources at accelerating rates and not replenishing them. The result is a burnout of our adrenals and other glands, a diminishment of nervous system function and depletion registered as continuing levels of exhaustion.

It's become the new norm when someone asks how we're doing to tell them how busy and full-tilt our lives are. Going at a fast rate, with a long list of to-dos and feeling fairly overwhelmed, is now a part of our standard experience and a cultural norm. We live over-stimulated lives, and there's less and less time to experience the inner quiet aspect of our self, to tap into what we're really feeling. Instead, we ricochet around like pinballs from one call to attention to the next, with no downtime in between. This is a formula for breakdown, overloading the body to the point where it does not have the resources to maintain even basic health, and this can open the door for disease to enter.

We have to have time, space and nutrients to restore what has been expended for the body to maintain its function. When challenges are not resolved, to some degree, our nervous system does not return to a resting state. Somewhere, an issue is on hold in our nervous system registry. With this, there is less rebuilding and repair. Our bodies are designed to resolve stressors and then return to a relaxed parasympathetic state that attends to repair and renewal. Less downtime leads to greater toxicity being held within and with it, greater risk of disease. We live lives that are constantly 'turned on.' We are barraged by sensory stimulation, much of it made available via our electronic devices, as well as electromagnetic energies that cause our bodies stress.

We're constantly in contact with electronics now that smartphones are universal. They are now growing at a rate of sales of 1.5 billion new devices worldwide per year! People go from screen to screen, one electronic device to another. Our bodies try and tune us to what is in our environment, just as in previous times humanity was more 'tuned' with the sun and moon and earth rhythms. We're far healthier when we have more natural 'tuning' than when we are mostly exposed to electronics.

If we are sleeping less—and as a population we are, since insomnia is a growing issue—then not only are our bodies becoming more exhausted from the lack of rest, but also less detox is occurring. Sleep is a time when the body does much-needed maintenance and restores itself. With the toxicity level increasing and the rest and renewal time decreasing, this creates another challenge for the body to handle, as its resources to adequately clear toxins are decreased while the load is increasing.

We need to 'reset our clock' internally, by being more active while the sun is up and paying attention to systems of ancient wisdom that suggest that it is good to allow time for slowing down and relaxing in preparation for rest. It's not reasonable to think that quality sleep will follow from staying 'on'—having our brain activated doing something on the computer or using the light stimulation that iPads and smartphones offer, while having them in bed with us to the end of our day. Writer John Sutter makes this point in an article about the effect of electronic devices on our body rhythms:

> When receptors in our eyes are hit with bright light for an extended period of time, they send a message to the brain saying it's time to be awake. The brain, in turn, stops secreting a hormone called melatonin, which makes people sleepy and helps regulate the internal sleep clock.

John Sutter makes the point that by positioning ourselves in front of these electronic devices that project quite a bit of blue light into the evening and night hours, we're receiving strong signals to be active at a time when our internal clock is trying to help us wind down. If we want our bodies to be properly 'tuned' and holding the proper circadian rhythms for health, we have to go outside and receive some rays of sunshine, and with it, vitamin D, during the day as much as possible. This little vitamin has been discovered to have a multitude of roles to orchestrate health in the body, including helping our immune system to function properly. We also need to go outside to get the blue light of the day to regulate our bodies for health.

These words of understanding come from Dr. Stone: "A simple lily in the field is arrayed in its natural beauty because of its uninterrupted rhythmic energy supply, in tune with nature." Although we have become very adept as a species in creating manmade environments that offer plentiful enjoyment for living in many ways, it doesn't mean that we have trumped ancient biological systems design. We need daily doses of nature and its good influence on our biological systems to maintain balance and harmony.

Toxins, Hydration and the Lymph

The quote below from Dr. Haas, sums up the scenario we face:

> Toxicity is of much greater concern…than ever before. There are many new and stronger chemicals, air and water pollution, radiation and nuclear power. We ingest new chemicals, use more drugs of all kinds, eat more sugar and refined foods, and daily abuse ourselves with various stimulants and sedatives. The incidence of many toxicity diseases has increased as well. Cancer and cardiovascular disease are two of the main ones.

Arthritis, allergies, obesity, and many skin problems are others. In addition, a wide range of symptoms, such as headaches, fatigue, pains, coughs, gastrointestinal problems, and problems from immune weakness, can all be related to toxicity.

The human lymph is a very intelligent and well-designed system, but the level of toxins we breathe in, consume and absorb—often unknowingly—is beyond what any body system has been designed to handle. The Environmental Protection Agency prepares a report each year known as the Toxic Release Inventory (TRI). This report is its best data on the amount of toxic chemical waste that was disposed of or released directly into the environment without treatment. In 2013, combined reports showed that 4.14 billion pounds were disposed of without treatment. While the air polluted by toxic waste has gone down in recent years, the overall amount of toxic chemical waste has continued to increase. This staggering number shows that each day we are exposed to an unprecedented level of toxicity because these toxins are going into our air, water and land, and some amount of this is being dumped directly into our bodies as a result.

Most of us don't know how very vital minerals are, not only directly to build health, but to decrease toxicity. Not only are our bodies more toxic, processing toxins causes the body to use up important minerals in order to neutralize and release them. One common example comes from drinking soda. One standard 12-ounce cola drink can take up to 100 mg of the alkaline mineral calcium to buffer. This is just one example of how the Standard American Diet causes the body to suffer from acidic pH.

We are living with fewer minerals coming to us in our foods because of how our soils are treated; much of agriculture uses imbalanced mineral elements to jumpstart growth of crops, without regard to the overall health of the soil. More research is showing that soil health corresponds with health in the body because food is the source of many vital nutrients needed to stay strong. In addition, our current fixation on and addiction to sugar is another way that important minerals, such as calcium, are used to balance the overly acidic condition that sugar-laden foods create, thus decreasing the level of vital nutrients needed by the body to maintain a state of health.

Our ancestors had to deal with saber-tooth tigers. When a predator leapt at you, it was quite visible. Now one of our greatest threats is the deluge of toxins that are mostly invisible to our view. Yet these toxins are a real threat that takes a toll day by day as they build up inside. Often, though, we don't really notice that our function is diminishing until our symptoms increase dramatically. We don't know that the toxin level has reached a critical threshold until some kind of major condition presents itself. By realizing what we need at the cellular level, we can begin to take corrective measures daily to restore more health and greater well-being.

As long ago as the early twentieth century, Dr. Alex Carrel won the Nobel Prize in Physiology or Medicine for his research revealing the immortality of the cell. He was successful in keeping tissues and organs alive for years by continually supplying needed nutrients and clearing away wastes. More than a hundred years ago now, his research showed that cells can have a long life if provided the necessities and adequate waste disposal. Dr. Carrel also showed that it didn't take but minute amounts of poisonous substances to filtrate the blood and fluids before balance was disturbed and aging began.

Signs of Sluggish Lymph

Under normal conditions, the lymph moves slowly through its one-way system of channels, so we don't want anything to reduce this level of circulation. Given present-day conditions, we really need to augment the circulation of lymph regularly in order to help the body stay ahead of the deluge of toxins.

Below is a list of symptoms that can be indications that the lymph is not flowing or able to work effectively on the body's behalf. It makes the point that if the waste removal system isn't working well it can result in a lot of uncomfortable symptoms.

- Decreased immune function, i.e., recurring colds and flu
- Headaches
- Stuffy sinuses
- Continuing infections of ears, throat, lungs
- Ongoing catarrh conditions
- Swelling in the lymph nodes
- Disturbed sleep
- Nausea, bloating, gas, constipation
- Acid reflux or indigestion
- Inability to lose weight
- Low backache
- Stiff joints
- Fatigue, low energy and exhaustion
- Skin outbreaks, rashes, dry or itchy skin
- Nervousness, fear, anxiety
- Lack of concentration
- Feeling depressed and low
- Frequent mood swings

It's interesting that this list corresponds in great measure with lymph researcher John Ossipinski's list for indications of inner tissue acidosis. These conditions are indications that suggest a need for more alkalinity and circulation to provide the necessary environment for healthy lymph system function. This list clearly indicates that the lymph has system-wide symptoms when it is blocked or stagnant that can be physical, mental and emotional.

The lymph fluids are a vast inner system to bathe the cells with water and nutrients and take away the waste so the cells can thrive. As with a polluted lake, we need forms of remediation to help our inner fluids when they become acidic and the vessels and nodes congested. Water that is full of toxins and has become acidic causes damage to the life within it. Our fluids are much more effective when they are oxygenated and alkaline so that cells can thrive, and we feel much more alive and energetic. At the micro level, the cells are meant to have the right volume of fluids with a friendly chemical composition surrounding them, helping them to remain flexible and permeable so they can receive nutrients and let go of waste.

Ancient healing wisdom makes the point that, to age well, we must be proactive in taking care of ourselves. We may become passive or fatalistic about letting life take its course, but we need to live in a way that is an antidote to all the toxic exposure, by taking positive action.

There is some good news to counter the disturbing reality of continuing toxic deluge; there are lots of advances in the public perception about what to do about health, and there are now lots of detox protocols and products that are effective. Most protocols are aimed at cleansing the intestines, liver, kidneys or skin, and to some degree they work to assist the lymph system, because it is so interrelated with these other body systems that also work to detox on our behalf. Yet we have not yet realized that in order to be healthy, we have to be educated about this major behind-the-scenes ally that we are all born with and learn to support its work to help us function optimally. Otherwise, our health can easily spiral downwards into some form of degenerative condition, and with it, our life focus narrows to deal with a major healing crisis..

Surprisingly, the greatest volume of water in us is mostly lymph. It is about double the fluid volume of the blood. The lymph system is a vast low pressure hydraulic system designed to internally bathe our bodies using the cleansing and healing power of water. Yet our modern lifestyle is dehydrating. According to the formulator of the Cell Food trace mineral products, Dr. David Dyer, "Dehydration causes bodily functions to go into distress, because fewer toxins are being removed, and less oxygen and nutrients can be transported throughout the body—especially the brain, which is about 80 to 90% water."

Another consideration for the effect of dehydration comes from Dr. Fereydoon Batmanghelidj, who indicates that the right volume of water (hydration) helps the proteins and enzymes in the body to function better. The lymph is slightly viscous, but the thicker it becomes, the less efficient proteins and enzymes are. In addition, the right amount of water helps all the elements in the structure of the cell, including its receptors, to function properly and cohere as a unit.

Stress takes a toll on the body's ability to use its fluids for basic life functions. Two mainstays of modern-day living, sugar and caffeine, are highly dehydrating, moving the body away from the level of hydration that is needed to preserve its function. Fast foods, processed foods and rich foods all require enormous quantities of the body's water reserves to process internally. We misinterpret many of the body's signals for water as a reason to eat, adding food into the system when hydration is what is being called for. We have a plethora of health conditions, and at their core, there is a high correspondence with an increasing deficiency of water within.

Dr. Batmanghelidj was the author of a paradigm-changing book called *Your Body's Many Cries for Water.* After working to clinically resolve a host of different kinds of conditions, he came to the conclusion that chronic water dehydration was at the root of most disease states. This book presents Dr. Batmanghelidj's work showing how disconnected we have become from one of the basic needs of life. If we are born with a water volume between 70-75% but shrink down to as low as the fifty percent range toward the end of life, does it not make sense that body systems are designed to function at their best with an adequate to optimal volume of water?

The lymph system is just slightly less than a 100% fluid reservoir. If this key system is designed to use the medium of water to cleanse and heal and renew and nourish, then what can we say about putting our body system in a continuing state of crisis, having to constantly ration water to the most critical functions while curtailing water flow to other parts of the body?

[2]
Improving Lymph Function

Stay Hydrated

In order for this magnificent system to function well, we should drink half of our weight in fluid ounces each day. If we are exercising or spend time outside in heat or in a sauna, then this number goes up. Caffeinated and sugary beverages don't count toward this basic threshold of daily water intake. Therein lies the problem. In our modern-day development, we have cultivated a taste for drinks that are daily deepening the water shortage within.

It's best to develop a habit of drinking some sort of pure water, without heavy metals and toxins in it. Also know that if you wait until you're thirsty, the body is already slightly dehydrated. Signals from within that are meant to get us to drink are often misinterpreted to eat more or drink more dehydrating drinks, when we actually need more water for adequate hydration.

One of the best practices to help our bodies to cleanse is to drink a couple of glasses of water each day upon waking. Overnight the body has been doing its work of detox, and if upon waking we rehydrate, it gives this clearing process a boost because we're bringing the volume of hydration up to allow the body to complete its work. Being hydrated provides an added benefit so that you feel more focused in the morning and can start the day more productively without the need for caffeine to jolt the body into being able to function.

The book *Water and Salt: The Essence of Life* provides great information about the uses of water for healing. For better absorption and function within, this book suggests making a solution called sole simply by infusing Himalayan rock salt crystals in water. I make it by placing a couple of the salt crystals into about a cup of water in a glass jar with a lid. Then I let it dissolve for a couple of hours. Once the water is saturated with salt, the crystals will not break down any further into the solution, so there should be a bit of crystal left in the water. This indicates that it has reached the 26% salt saturation level. This solution has many uses, but for the topic of hydration, a little of this solution added to good water will do wonders, softening the water so that it actually rolls on the tongue.

The author of the book, Dr. Barbara Hendel, is a German naturopathic doctor who uses this form of water therapy. In her book she suggests beginning the day with a teaspoon of sole in a glass of pure spring water on an empty stomach. So far, I've found that a mere drop (seriously, one drop) of this solution in a quart of water (this is what I put in my own daily water jar) significantly changes the texture and taste of the water for the better, while boosting its cleansing ability. She clearly indicates that it is not the quantity but the regularity of taking in some of the sole that boosts the body's ability because of the bioenergy that is released from this combination in solution.

The salt crystal immediately helps the water to be structured in a way that is good for the body. This is no ordinary salt, stripped of its natural composition and capacity. When an intact crystal of mineral salt and water combine, the synergy of the two forms a solution with more bioenergy available to detox and return the body to more equilibrium.

As an example of the potency of water combined with salt, the life-germinating sperm cell is composed of 99% water and 1% salt! Like the great mother water oceans and seas that cover most of this planet, tiny little sperm are profound catalysts for the creation of new life!

Many have written of the similarity between the composition of the blood within us and ocean water. Sole is an ocean-like solution with many properties that help to restore more vital rhythms within. This kind of water solution has more capacity than standard water. It is recommended to drink this water regularly and to only add enough sole to boost the cleansing power of the water to a comfortable level.

Because modern-day eating and habits contribute to a buildup of toxins and the effects of partially decomposed and fermented waste products, this solution will bring a powerful boost to your water, restoring it to its natural potency. You may feel energized from the combination of water with a tiny addition of this powerful form of natural salt. It can greatly assist the body in its work of detox, helping to loosen deposits of toxic debris so it can be cleared through the intestinal system. This water is potent in its ability to get things to move and catalyze clearing, so if you try it, only use a drop for the first week, as you notice what happens. Then add more drops as it feels right in your health regimen.

Like any detox, if it gets going faster than is comfortable to handle, stop for a day or two. While a healing crisis can help to move a lot out in a short period of time, slow and steady really is more enjoyable and has very long-lasting good results. The sole-infused water is liquid and smooth and feels tastier and more enjoyable than even pure bottled standard spring water on its own.

A local water store where I live uses trace minerals in its purified water, and this water too is quite smooth, because the minerals help the water to be structured. David, the store owner, also uses magnets on the water system, which also helps to structure the water. There are even some home systems that make use of magnets to help structure the water. This trace mineral water promotes some good cleansing action, so I've learned not to overdo it. It's actually interesting to find protocols that work to assist the body in its work without overdoing the effects and keep adding in what works to realize more optimal functioning. Experimenting keeps things fresh and engages the mind's participation in the process of it all, enjoying and appreciating the process of unfolding and observing the body's wisdom in action.

As a connoisseur of water, I've sought out the best-tasting pure water from places in nature, including a well on the property of a friend's home in Santa Fe, a spring in the Hocking Hills of southern Ohio, and an artesian bottled water from Idaho, sold as Trinity, three personal bests. (Trinity is no longer available.) Now I've found a bottled water from an artesian source in Jana, Croatia, that is particularly pleasing to my water palate for special treats. While water is universal, it isn't all the same. When water is full of chemicals, it loses much of its own innate power to heal, cleanse and support systems to function optimally within.

On the journey to become more aligned with our inner fluid system of lymph, the largest internal water reservoir, it is good to begin really considering what kind of water we're taking in and begin to notice how we feel when we drink water, as well as to notice the different effects that can come from special water sources. Water is a ubiquitous aspect of life, and because it is always there, we can take it for granted and overlook its primary importance in our lives. In learning to value the lymph system, we will simultaneously be orienting to water's ability to hydrate for the body to function well.

Adding a bit of lemon gives the water a more alkalizing effect and increases the capacity to clear unwanted toxins. You can add a bit of something like liquid stevia if it tastes too sour. Other tasty additions include cucumber slices, limes or oranges, to infuse a bit of taste into water and increase its palate appeal and reinforce the habit of hydrating in a natural way.

A widely recommended protocol in the detox and healthy living communities is to have warm lemon water upon waking. Squeeze up to half a lemon into warm water and drink like a tea, first thing. This combination is an alkalizing boost that promotes intestinal peristalsis to help the body clear out after its nightly work to detox. The lemon also helps the liver to make bile, a body secretion that works to clear toxins from the body. Again, add some healthy sweetener, like stevia or honey, if you need to make it more palatable so it can become more of a habit.

The lemon water is a big boost for beginning the day in a good way, and the vitamin C in the lemon also helps the body to rid itself of debris, as it helps to boost the immune system, so beleaguered from toxins and stress. Lemon also supports more calm mentally. With lemon, it's a win-win all around.

Well known author and nutritionist Ann Louise Gittleman, of the *Fat Flush Plan* and other proactive health guides, has recommended use of cranberry juice to flush the lymph system by breaking up deposits (especially fat) in the lymph nodes and ducts. Because the lymph system is the major transport for fats that we ingest from the intestines back to the blood circulatory system, the system can become clogged with these large molecules when it is hampered in its ability to move these internal fluids.

The standard American diet, unfortunately, is filled with many bad fats and not enough of those that the body really needs, like omega-3 fatty acids needed for cellular health and brain function. In America, we tend to get too many omega-6 oils (up to twenty times the required amount) and not enough of the more healthful omega-3s that are really good for maintaining the structure of the cell membrane.

Deposits, much of which are fat and protein, are a major reason why the lymph system does not function well. This is where a good digestive enzyme can really make a difference in how well the lymph system can function through boosting the body's ability to digest these much-needed food substances rather than becoming a load for the lymph to dispose of. Clogged lymph can lead to degenerative issues because of toxic buildup, diminished immune function and the decreased ability of the lymph to provide fluid circulation that will cleanse the cell waste to keep our systems vital.

Gittleman's protocol recommends using pure cranberry juice, not a blend, added to good water. She recommends taking 8 ounces of the juice and adding water to make 64 ounces to drink throughout the day. The fruit acids, enzymes and flavonoids (plant pigment micronutrients) have been proven to support lymph function. The catalytic power of the cranberry's fruit acids and other compounds work to free up trapped fatty deposits in the nodes and make the fluid less thick with undigested debris. Gittleman says that up to fifteen pounds of waste-filled water can then be flushed out, because the body has more of what it needs to clear itself. In taking in cranberry, I certainly have noticed more water leaving!

This cran-water drink also assists the liver in its work to detox. The liver is overburdened from modern-day toxic input, so this practice is a simple and effective way to hydrate and gently detox daily that benefits both the lymph and its companion organ, the liver. It will bring many benefits to boost your body to be more effective and look and feel better in the process.

Another great way to maintain a better fluid balance within is to drink a couple of glasses of water before heading out for a heavy dinner, party or any ingestion of alcoholic beverages. This doesn't really count toward the basic daily fluid requirement, but it will help your system to handle the influx of substances that require more work to process and are dehydrating in nature. There is an immediate benefit to this practice, you can enjoy celebrating without so many negative after-effects that occur from dehydration. The general consensus is that water is best before meals, not during or shortly after, so as to keep from interfering with digestion.

Did you know that being properly dehydrated will deter many headaches or that feeling tired is often a sign of being somewhat dehydrated? As adults we become used to being slightly dehydrated and usually don't realize that we're not only sacrificing the capacity of the lymph system, but also decreasing the function of other bodily systems and, with it, our fluid system capacity that is the basis of cleansing and renewal within. When we are born, we are 70% or more composed of water, so it is a major foundation of life.

Many beverages in the modern world are dehydrating and acidic in their pH, and they are what most of us use as our daily fluid intake. In order to be healthy, we really must turn this around and become a nation of water drinkers that are providing the basis for the body to cleanse itself and be more alkaline, as it is intended to be. Adequate water intake keeps us fluid so that we can meet life's challenges and be focused, productive and healthy. The old saying that "health is our greatest wealth" is a worthwhile focus for our proactive initiatives.

Less Acid More Alkaline

So many experts have spoken of the need to move away from our highly acidic way of eating that it should be understood as commonly as the ills of smoking, yet it is not. The Standard American Diet (SAD) is filled with processed and fast foods. This is a formula for losing health and vitality as a trade-off for enjoying the intake of substances that are common, familiar and, too often, toxic and addictive. The American dependence on sugar can be traced to a shift in the food industry decades ago. It responded to a consumer concern and cut fat in its products. In order to maintain food appeal the industry shifted to adding sugar in its products.

What has been the result of these changes? The average intake of sugar in America rose 39% from the 1950s to 2000. According to the USDA, consumption rose from 109 pounds per year on average to 152 pounds per year during this period. As a highly acid-forming substance, this is a large burden for the body to be challenged to buffer.

While studies show there has been a decline from its record high in 1999, according to a study reported in the JAMA Internal Medicine journal in 2014, 71.4% of Americans were taking in more than 10% of their daily calorie intake from sugar through a combination of food and drinks. Most of this added sugar came from soda drinks. It is now well known that high sugar intake is related to many of the common degenerative diseases of our time: high blood pressure, high cholesterol, cardiovascular disease and diabetes.

Related to Americans' soda intake, Dr. Stone, a health visionary of his time, taught his students about the dangers of carbon dioxide drinks (the soda ingredient that gives it that enjoyable fizz) and the toll it takes on the body, as it has to manage storage of this gas in its tissues. Recall, carbon dioxide is what the body *releases* after proper metabolism as a waste gas. It is not a substance we want to increase for a healthy inner terrain.

Dr. Stone recognized the problem with soda from one standpoint. Soda brings up another problem that is rampant today: our eating choices are too acidic for the body. We are mostly water, and pure water is neutral on the scale of pH, measured as a 7. Our blood is best kept within an alkaline pH range of 7.35 to 7.45, and most of our tissues function best in the alkaline range, except the specialized tissues and organs involved in digesting.

Drinking a beverage with a pH of 6 doesn't sound like it's all that much different from a neutral pH. Yet when we drink a liquid with a pH of 6, this liquid is ten times more acidic than neutral water, because the scale has "a 10-fold difference between each number." If a liquid has a pH of 5, then it is one hundred times more acidic than water! Many waters on the market that are sold as 'healthy' are often 'purified' city water that do not have a pH even close to 7.

Well, it gets even worse. Sodas can have a pH of merely 3, which is very highly acidic. With the way that pH measurement works, this would mean that a soda is exposing the body to acidic conditions that are 10,000 times more acidic than water. This is a serious hit for the body to take and maintain a healthy equilibrium. The word equilibrium is used here to make the point that the body has to make many adjustments to balance all the various ways that we are alive and actively metabolizing. There are naturally many acidic results from daily metabolism that have to be buffered with alkaline minerals to maintain the right conditions for our cells to function. When our way of life is consistently harmful, it can put our health in jeopardy.

As an example, since I've known about how bad soda is to the body and our fluid equilibrium for a long time, I used the information to wean myself off this bad habit begun in early childhood. I drank a small pond of Coke while growing up. Recently, the point was made in a very stark manner when a neighbor showing signs of addiction to soda—his apartment was filled with stacked large plastic bottles of it— was diagnosed with an advanced brain tumor.

Qigong master Chunyi Lin has said that too much acid energy in the brain slowly shuts it down. Whatever the specific cause for the neighbor's brain tumor, none of us wants to face such devastation. Whether this habit was a cause or a contributor to disease in his case, the point for us all is to be proactive in course-correcting our choices to align with living vibrantly. It's worth facing the challenge of change to become more authentic and fulfilled.

One of the reasons that soda is so unbalanced is because of the sugar, a highly acidic substance that has another deleterious effect on the body: it requires precious resources, the alkaline minerals, to be pulled from wherever they are available to buffer the effects of this substance. These alkaline minerals then are not available for regular maintenance functions elsewhere in the body, like the alkaline liquid lymph system's fluid balancing work that is so critical to our health.

One of the major minerals of the body is calcium. This mineral, according to Dr. Gabriel Cousens, is used to foster the body's vitality, build strong bones and teeth and help to keep us calm, among many other functions. We don't realize that we are expending these important resources—actually squandering them in ways that erode our ability to functionlet alone live well.

Because we have a much smaller percentage of minerals in our food than we did before developing our highly industrialized form of agriculture, as well as our acidic food preferences, the body is giving up minerals that may already be in too short supply to buffer this intake. It is very stressful to the body operation to have to apportion minerals in short supply. Our modern day 'advances' in making 'food' widely available have traded real living foods with much needed nutrition for those with an extended shelf life and flavor appeal.

Dr. Cousens has stated that neither our soil nor the food grown in it has enough available mineral nutrients to create cell health. Standard processed food has even fewer mineral nutrients available. This deficiency of available minerals, he has written, is a major reason why cells become weaker and more vulnerable to opportunistic invaders, such as some forms of bacteria, fungus, viruses and many forms of parasites. He writes of needing angstrom-sized (very small) particles that are water-soluble to be most available for the body's use.

The health and function of our lymph system is critical, because we cannot live if it becomes so clogged and polluted that it can't do its job. When our body becomes increasingly acidic, the tissue also becomes tighter as toxins take their toll internally. This form of toxicity, otherwise known as acidosis or congestion, impairs the ability of the body's vital systems to function. Without the work of the lymph as a master regulator, we cannot expect our bodies to function well, or possibly at all. These inner fluids are key to our life and health.

When the body is increasingly acidic, systems become sluggish, the volume of oxygen is lower and microbes tend to proliferate. This is a description of a system prone to some kind of degenerative condition because of the decreased viability of our cells to live in a polluted environment. Cells are the building blocks of tissues and organ systems within. Minerals are building blocks of the cells, along with water. We cannot live without our cells, so we need to give them more natural substances with nutrients intact for the cells to be functional and healthy. Instead of a lot of heavy processed food, the body is in need of foods high in antioxidants, such as cranberries and raspberries, as well as cleansing green vegetables to counter the cell-damaging effects of free radicals from both our basic metabolic processes and unhealthy substances we consume.

Whether tightness in the body comes from acidic conditions or stress (also an acidifying influence), acidic pH also restricts the lymph vessels, and this hampers movement of these fluids. So while there is pressure on the body because of the increased acid intake to perform more work, it is simultaneously becoming less capable of handling the load due to congestion in the lymph. This reservoir of fluid must have a certain capacity to both carry away waste and bring nutrients. When it is filled with acidic toxins, this ability is hindered in great measure, and this can lead to some very deleterious outworking.

A long standing program that has done much to reverse seemingly intractable heart and cardiovascular issues was spawned by the renowned Dr. Dean Ornish more than three decades ago. Two of the major tenets of his program are based on using real foods as well as physical activity to promote proper circulation. For thirty-five years, Dr. Ornish has helped to save countless lives by teaching people that it is worth the investment to make changes that promote quality of life and longevity.

Lymph educator, advocate and bodywork expert John Ossipinsky has rightly described the lymph as "the other circulatory system," since one of its main jobs is to return fluids that have leaked from the arterial capillaries back to the venous system after doing some important work for the body. John Ossipinki's comment is very perceptive; there is a yin and yang to the lymph and the blood circulatory systems; one completes the other to make a larger whole.

This other circulatory system also needs real food to maintain the proper pH so that it can continue its vital work for the body. When the body is able to remove metabolic debris because the lymph is functioning, then key life-giving nutrients can flow into the cells, completing one of the major goals of fluid circulation in the body. It is time that we recognize how vital and interdependent the blood and lymph fluid systems are for our life and well-being.

Dr. Ornish is a medical pioneer who has helped to reconnect Western medicine with its life-affirming Hippocratic oath. Now there are many other medical and health experts acting as effective guides to demonstrate that our lifestyle is a direct contributor to the chemical composition within our body. It's time we heed the expert advice and move our chemistry in a more alkaline and life-promoting direction.

The Inner Terrain, Still a New Frontier

The terrain...is everything.

Claude Bernard

The quote above is from French physiologist Claude Bernard, a contemporary of Louis Pasteur. Pasteur acknowledged Bernard's contribution at the end of his life, in essence debunking his own theory of germs as the major causal force in disease. Yet the Western world had already embraced this idea, and it has remained firmly rooted in the collective as a belief for far too long. Claude Bernard, Dr. Alex Carrel and René Quinton were all scientists who made great contributions to understand that the inner bio-terrain is the prime cause for either life and health or disease and degeneration.

French research scientist and physiologist René Quinton demonstrated that indeed, 'terrain is everything.' He had theorized that, in order for a species to make the transition from ocean to land, it had to take its own life-supporting solution with it internally in order to survive.

René Quinton was working on his major research from 1897 until his death in 1925. Prior to the work of Quinton, as early as the 1750s, an English physician, Dr. Richard Russell, had developed a protocol of drinking seawater and bathing in ocean water to treat enlarged lymph nodes. Through decades of clinical practice, René Quinton came to the conclusion that a very special solution existed within certain vortex zones of the ocean that maintained a potency to overcome shortcomings in human genetics. Quinton proved that the right fluid—in this case, a specific vortex ocean plasma substance that first came to be known as Quinton Plasma—could overcome genetic abnormalities in thousands of cases involving babies born with severe birth defects.

René Quinton helped thousands of pregnant women with a previous history of miscarriage to have healthy babies. According to Oriental Medical Doctor (OMD) Roy Dittman, through the use of Quinton Plasma, René Quinton

> …successfully helped hundreds of thousands of people suffering from a mind-boggling array of health challenges related to a deficient bio-terrain. The list of conditions positively impacted by treatment with Quinton Plasma goes on and on.

> Why? Because Marine Plasma is the quintessential solution for homeostasis; it is nature's argument for bio-terrain theory.

During his lifetime, René Quinton was a decorated hero in France for his clinical work, and he was hailed as a new 'Louis Pasteur.' His findings were highly effective for decades in eradicating a wide array of diseases before the first antibiotic was discovered in 1928. Quinton was even invited to Egypt, where this special marine plasma was used to save thousands of lives.

According to René Quinton, this "original" biological terrain "is our single most enduring physiological trait." This "ground substance" is a biological inheritance that is 2.5 billion years old. The reason that this particular marine plasma fluid proved to be so potent in its ability to restore health is that our human biological terrain—the interior ocean of plasma that bathes our trillions of cells—is actually quite similar to the saline ocean that covers much of the earth. It is so similar that it has been used to completely replace plasma in some mammals without injury or death. The French used Quinton marine solution during the war for transfusions as a protocol because it was so effective.

OMD Roy Dittman has written that

> Everything in the human body responds to the condition of our extra-cellular fluid–the 'sea aquarium' or 'marine terrain' as René Quinton often referred to it. It is the microcosm of the sea itself. When you restore the quality of this internal sea aquarium to its original marine inheritance, every cell, organ, and tissue begins to respond and function as it was intended.

In looking at the profile of Original Quinton, extra-cellular fluid (from which lymph is formed), and blood plasma, the proportions of key minerals in solution are very similar.

Despite these impressive findings and extensive clinical results from René Quinton, in modern-day America, our inner fluid terrain is largely a vast ocean of uncharted water within. There has been a collective interest in the health-conscious community to improve the purity and quantity of our water intake. This is to be applauded since it's so important to the quality of the inner bio-terrain. Yet the increase in degenerative diseases in the Western world points to some kind of disharmony in the ecology of our inner terrain, which is mostly fluid. We are too acidic from having an imbalance of food and toxins (and sometimes even water) whose pH makes it difficult for the cells, the basic biological units within our body, to remain viable and healthy.

We need to learn more about protecting and preserving the living solution of our inner terrain. Some doctors in Western medicine have begun to study this, as they have realized more finely that, at its core, disease is a system-wide issue. Eastern healing systems, such as Tibetan and Chinese medicine and Ayurveda, have spoken to the importance of maintaining inner harmony and balance for ages, and these systems have some level of recognition that the inner terrain is a result of all that occurs—emotions and thoughts, as well as the food we eat, the water we drink and the external environment around us, for good or ill.

A yogi himself, Dr. Stone taught that the highest form of yoga was right thought. Thought has an impact upon the inner chemistry. All of the energy exchanges we have are part of the matrix that is our inner terrain. For health, longevity and happiness, realizing a commitment to fostering living vibrancy within is one of the most important actions that we can take.

Dr. Simon Yu, a Western medical doctor who combines Eastern and alternative protocols, has cited a French study from the 1950s that correlated water quality with high cancer rates in particular regions. "They found these regions often had one common denominator: poor water quality. Water was contaminated, oxidized, and acidic and found to block the body's metabolic detoxification." We know from a long history of science, beginning with Dr. Carrel's experiments more than one hundred years ago that if the cells are bathed in the right solution, they can live almost indefinitely. With the wrong solution, our inner terrain will be degraded, and signs of aging and disease will result.

Water is a universal healer and cleanser, and it is also a medium and a messenger that helps our body to access the right information on how to function. An excellent example of water's role comes from, Dr. Haas; "Fluids serve as the transmission and delivery device for the immune system." The body can only do its work well when we have the right electrical capacity from being hydrated internally with a volume of water and minerals in solution that the body's cells can utilize. Just as bodies of water on the earth with the right ecology allow many life forms to flourish, our inner ocean of fluid plasma has optimal chemistry when made of the right elements.

The Quinton marine plasma has clinically demonstrated that providing the right inner plasma solution, composed of alkalizing water and minerals in solution, allows the body to access more of its full genetic potential and promote vitality in life that can effectively counteract many significant degenerative conditions. Because the composition of the inner fluid terrain is central to the body's capacity to maintain health, we need to learn how to nourish and regenerate this basic matrix of life.

Eat Fresh, Organic, Unprocessed Foods

Since the lymph system is charged with clearing toxins, it makes sense to begin to make changes that will decrease the detox load that the lymph system must haul away. With the speed of life, we have become a nation of fast food eaters, using processed foods with abandon. We are eating food that is highly acidic, and this is an open invitation for degenerative disease to set in.

We need to be eating food that the body can recognize and process effectively, without becoming bogged down from the work to digest it. The body needs nutrition to function, and the lymph is being handicapped by an increase in toxic and degraded food intake, while simultaneously decreasing the nutrient substance needed to maintain basic health. At the micro level of our inner terrain, if we are eating and living in a way that promotes an acidic condition internally, then it actually slows movement of the fluid out of the cell. This is critical because it effectively limits the cell from receiving life-nourishing nutrients. The lymph is meant to provide a surrounding bath of fluid with enough alkaline minerals to keep the exchange going. Cells can suffocate and die if they are not able to receive life-giving supplies of oxygen and nutrients.

The inner terrain is basically invisible to us, so we don't know the toll that some of our choices are taking. While it might be invisible, it's also critical, since this biological solution really is the foundation for our health and longevity. The ancient system of Ayurveda called it 'longevity juice' for a good reason.

Nutritionist Ann Louise Gittleman makes the point that the body, including the liver, is well designed for detox, but it has to have a nutrient-dense diet to perform its work. The problem is, most diets aren't nutrient-dense; they are denatured, meaning that many of the basic nutrients have been filtered out and altered through processing.

Some of the best foods for the lymph system are ones that help us to stay hydrated—for example, fruits and veggies that are high in water content and free from toxins. The enzymes and acids available from raw fruit, eaten by itself or in a juice, are potent support for the work of lymph cleansing.

Soups are another great way to introduce hydrating food into the body, especially since we eat so many things like chips, fried food, pasta and bread products that take a lot of the body's water to balance the internal effect. Soup is an easy way to get a good mix of vegetables while using herbs and spices that are also lymph-friendly.

It's rather difficult to accept, but in the U.S., we no longer have food security. The 'food' we eat is mostly grown in an industrialized manner, with practices adopted for yield over nutrition or, for that matter, consumer safety. In order to maintain some kind of balance with health, we have to become daily advocates who read labels before we buy and stay somewhat abreast of the better known threats to safety with the food choices we are making.

As a nation, we need to become more involved in the choices we make and learn more about where our food comes from. For this reason, it is suggested to do as much eating of locally grown, organic and seasonal food as possible, so you can have a more direct relationship with what you're eating. If consumers do this, we will begin to alter the tide away from food that is not grown in a transparent manner and has hidden drawbacks that are not in our best health interests to eat.

Here in So Cal, we have a newly launched farm-to-table restaurant, Boldo Bowl, which uses produce grown within a couple hundred miles of the restaurant in Santa Ana. It is so fresh that, when I eat there, my body is immediately happy from the opportunity to eat food that is so vital.

If your goal is longevity and having a life that is not forced to focus on health issues that arise and demand your full attention, it's best to begin as soon as possible to eat more fresh, organic produce. Finding dishes that you like is the key. The more that good food is palatable, the more it will be repeated. In the process of making changes, there's always a bit of a course correction for our taste buds, but over time, our tastes can change, and it's far better to be proactive than to get caught in a health issue or disease that demands radical change and enormous asset expenditure to stay alive.

People often say that they can't afford a healthier lifestyle, and I respond, can you *afford* ill health? Whether we are paying this cost ourselves or with the support of a health insurance program, the burden of covering these rising costs is not having a good overall effect on the economy or our lives. This is definitely a case where 'an ounce of prevention is worth a pound of cure.' Course correction is far easier than the toll it takes to restore ourselves from life-threatening situations.

Get Your Green

Many years ago when I lived in my native state of Ohio, I really missed the sunshine over the winter. To counter this, I grew wheatgrass on my porch. One day I proudly offered a glistening glass of the green potion from my harvest to my mother Vella, who retorted, "I don't do green!" Well, it sure got me to chortle, but truth be told, we both could have used more sunshine-infused greens to help us stay healthy through those long, gray winters. Green foods are potent alkalizers and are naturally detoxing. Beyond eating an array of salad greens, we need to incorporate many more servings of all kinds of greens into our diet to help our system to function better and improve vitality.

The chlorophyll in my wheat grass, as well as young grasses such as alfalfa and barley, help to stimulate hemoglobin production. The herbs parsley, basil, oregano, cilantro and many other green herbs are also a chlorophyll-rich way to provide tasty and healthy benefits for the body. A green herb that is a not yet well known, purslane, is the best plant source of omega-3 oils, so this little herb has a lot to offer. It is also a very tasty addition to salads and sandwiches and easy to grow.

Another great way to increase the nutrition of our choices is a good choice many of us already make: using a dressing made with olive oil. The olive oil increases the body's absorption of nutrients. For instance, it helps the body to extract the lycopene that tomatoes are known for. How good is that?

Many greens are a good source of magnesium, a mineral that is all-too-deficient in our standard American diet (SAD). It's interesting that green is associated with calming, and many studies have shown that offices with green views lessen stress. Well, magnesium-rich greens taken internally are also calming and relaxing and are much needed. If you're not getting enough green and your palate for green is not yet activated, then you might consider a good product, such as Natural Vitality's Calm magnesium products, to promote better sleep and more relaxed tissues to improve your health.

Green foods help us to feel vital and have more energy. They bring an infusion of nutrients that are key for body function. If you're like my mother, though, and green is not very palatable, you can still benefit your body with either tablets or capsules of green food. Green foods help to boost immune function and, like water, are excellent cleansers for the body. They can easily be blended into a smoothie to add good nutrition without the palate-pleasing question. Smoothies themselves are also a great way to increase the antioxidants in the diet and put a good dose of nutrient-rich substances into the body without sacrificing taste appeal and adding a lot of sugar.

A great green flesh food is the avocado; it delivers very healthy fats to the body and is quite filling. It can be used in a multitude of ways beyond its dressing atop a salad or the ever-popular guacamole. I've had it in chocolate pudding and green smoothies, and it is luscious and rich without the body clogging effect of unhealthy fried fat foods. The avocado is also a great way to get a healthy dose of daily magnesium.

Another magnesium-dense food is the pumpkin seed. It is high in vegetarian protein, and a half-cup brings close to a day's worth of recommended magnesium. It is also a good source of zinc, a catalyst for the body's immune function. Experimenting with foods t0 find new palate-pleasing recipes that work to promote health is a great way to stay ahead of the body's need for nutrient infusion in ways that are enjoyable and nourishing.

Drink your Meal

Our ways of dining involve many food choices that are dry, like chips, toast and crunchy foods, and often require a lot of the body's water to metabolize. Taking in nutrition while maintaining a fluid equilibrium is a major goal of supporting the lymph system. Smoothies can be more than swirled fruity water. Using a blender to do some of the work to break down the plant cell membranes gives the body some assistance in its work to digest so it can attend to other metabolic matters.

When we place highly nutritious food items in a blender jar, we can make a meal in a minute that can really support our system for many hours. Because water is naturally heavy, it helps to feel filled up for a while, without having to pack in a lot of calories that may need to be burned off later. Unlike many foods that have been highly altered in the process of manufacturing, blended smoothies are an easy way to give the body foods that it recognizes. And food preparation is fairly simple as long as the ingredients are on hand. I find that having a few recipes I like and keeping these staples available makes for quick preparation when time is short or I've worked until I'm *really* hungry.

One of my favorite ways to start the day is with a kefir or yogurt-based smoothie, with an antioxidant- and phytonutrient-rich mix of berries, a potassium-rich banana, a green powder mix, shilajit (an earthy plant-based mineral powder), liquid minerals, lecithin, beet powder and cinnamon. If I need a bit more protein to start the day, I add a scoop of the Sunwarrior protein powder (Warrior Blend Vanilla). It's raw, with a full vegetarian protein profile that includes pea, cranberry and hemp. Cranberry brings a nice boost, since it is a very potent plant to improve lymph function. (The recipe is in the Resources section.)

This smoothie is tasty, easy to digest and a very hydrating blend with a good mix of protein to the sweet of the fruit so that it doesn't spike blood sugar. The cinnamon is another way to balance this intake of sweet. I keep experimenting with the edge of a palate-pleasing berry sweetness, the tartness of the yogurt, mixed in with earthy notes from the cinnamon and shilajit.

Nutrient-filled blended smoothies can be easier on the body to digest and take in substances to actually build the body and give it what it needs. Dr. William Sears, a doctor in Southern California, has treated many patients using his own vegetarian protein-packed smoothie recipe to help people make changes in eating habits. Dr. Sears has found it works to help his patients lose weight, while maintaining a satisfying feeling of fullness.

One of the recipes that combine good antioxidants with those wonderful red lymph supportive foods is a beet blueberry smoothie. Beets are great for vascular and lymph health and provide energy. Blueberries are a tasty and choice antioxidant with brain-boosting abilities. The cashews provide about 5 grams of protein, so they are a good way to balance the sweetness of the beets and blueberries. Here's the recipe:

1 medium raw beet, cleaned and with skin

1 cup frozen blueberries

1/4 cup of cashews

1/2 cup almond milk

1 cup of water

1/8 tsp. stevia or 1 tbl. of honey or maple syrup

The recipe calls for a handful of ice, but I don't tend to add ice to my smoothies.

Food Experimenting Can Be Good For Your Health

Eating food can be an ongoing experiment in how to make or find palate-pleasing nutrition that is good and good for you. While we all have habits of taste that are not good for us, when we make the decision to play and discover as part of our growth, then we can undertake making food choices as part of a discovery process, not a daily mindless habit. Food creates a chemical broth inside us, so the better our choices, the greater our likelihood to create a harmonious living pond rather than an inner sludgy sewage site. When we decide to make food a journey of discovery, we can give ourselves permission to try things out, to say no to some things and yes to others, while we expand our horizons about how food helps to provide a platform for a fulfilled life.

Including a higher percentage of living foods is a good way to foster a more alkaline inner environment that has proper food substance for the body to navigate all that is needed for metabolism. Dr. Stone, the founder of polarity therapy, used food in this way to help the body cleanse itself of toxins while increasing vitality. One of his primary protocols was to use a good quality olive oil and lemon on a daily salad. Another way to eat while lightly cleansing is to use olive oil pesto (without cheese) on lightly steamed vegetables. These are very simple ways to add a life vitality factor to bring in nutrients while helping the body to clear itself of toxicity as part of its daily work.

Olive oil is a good source of polyphenols, plant substances that are known to promote longevity. Polyphenols have been the subject of increasing research and attention in the past twenty plus years, because these phytochemicals are sources of abundant micronutrients. Plants that have polyphenols are the most abundant source of antioxidants in our diet.

Present-day medical practitioner Dr. Sears makes the point that to function well we need to be eating the right oils. Too many of us don't even think that we are regularly ingesting oils that have been pumped full of chemicals and heated industrially to searing high temperatures for days before they are disposed of, as a primary source of dietary fat intake. Good oils are essential on the micro level for the body's cell membranes to be strong and pliable in order to function well.

Contrary to popular notions about food needing to be low-fat, the brain is a major body system that needs the right amount of good oils to function well, and the more unheated and unprocessed, the better. A couple of examples of the best oils for the body are found in wild salmon, olives, avocados, flax, chia, hemp and coconut. Walnuts are particularly good for the brain. Many nut oils are very good, but they may be high in omega-6s, so it is good to balance the ratio of omega-3 to 6 overall. Pumpkin seeds are high in beneficial oil that supports reproductive health in men. They are also a good source of the immune-boosting mineral zinc.

We need far more omega-3s in our diet and dramatically fewer omega-6s, as well as cutting back on highly heated and denatured oils. While I have dearly loved French fries throughout my life, they have become too costly to my system, so now I have found much better options to provide my body with fats that provide energy fuel and compounds to nourish my cell and brain function, like flax and chia seed oil. Baked sweet potato fries are a tasty and healthy way to avoid drenching vegetables in broiled fat for flavor.

A mix of chia oil omega-3, 6 and 9 oils with CoQ10 looks promising to bring more energy and the right proportions of the different fatty acids into the daily diet. Co-enzyme Q10 is a valuable substance made in the body that acts as an antioxidant and protects our cells. In this case the CoQ10 helps the omega oils remain good fats as they are transported and not become oxidized before the body can utilize them. As we age, we may not have enough to protect our cells, so supplementing can boost the body to have the antioxidant capacity it needs. (See the Resources section for more information.)

The lymph is a major transporter of fat (lipids) and fat-soluble vitamins in the body, moving these fatty substances from the lymph vessels known as lacteals in the intestines to the blood circulatory system. The lymph can become filled with undigested fat (some of it highly altered as part of processing, or as a fried fat), thus creating quite a burden on the body to deal with. In addition, the body stores toxins that it cannot eliminate in fat. Not only is our environment toxin drenched, chemicals are often found in commercial oils, making it even harder for the body to clear the degraded fat when it is filled with toxins. The process of improving lymph and bodily function can be vastly improved by reducing complicated and adulterated food choices. Rather than having to spend a lot of time focusing on detox to live, we need to be more proactive, allowing life to become simpler by eating more real and pure food that is pleasing to the evolving palate. When food has good taste appeal, we are much more likely to repeat the choice.

Hydrating Food

An innovative pioneer with raw food and spiritual development, Dr. Cousens has been merging spirit with a pure food diet for decades to promote conscious living and longevity. He was a pioneer in forwarding the idea that raw fruits and vegetables have a good quantity of what he calls "structured water." This is water that organized so that the body's cells can make use of it more readily.

More recently, a So Cal skin specialist, Dr. Howard Murad, has developed protocols for health involving hydration. A primary recommendation of his; 'cellular water boosters.' Dr. Murad has indicated, "When we eat this way, the body is flooded internally with micronutrients to create the ideal environment for the production of healthy cells." He underscores that eating hydrating foods doesn't make the body expend valuable resources as it does on digesting heavy foods that need lots of water to process. Eating hydrating foods helps the body to have the highly usable water it needs to keep cells hydrated and nourished with the abundance of antioxidants and anti-inflammatories found in living foods. "If you replace at least one glass of water a day with one serving of raw fruits or vegetables, you will be able to stay hydrated significantly longer."

This protocol dovetails with what Dr. Cousens has been teaching for many years: to use raw foods to boost the intake of water-based nutrients to support cell health and function. He was one of the first to note that hydrating foods, such as greens, increase the body's ability to transport much-needed nutrients to our cells to keep them healthy.

This way of eating foods that are already rich in structured water or cellular water boosters also supports the function of the water-based lymph system to have an adequate pure water volume to bathe the cells and carry away waste. The body has to have a significant intake of water to do its work properly and keep the cells healthy. One of the most important steps we can take is to begin to learn how to drink good, pure water and eat in a way that supports cell health and the work of our major water-based transport system, the lymph.

Some of the top foods for cellular health and lymph function include the cucumber, full of water (up to 96%) and the element silica, a potent building block of the body. Dr. Murad recommends the pomegranate, a juicy fruit that he indicates may be one of the highest sources of polyphenol antioxidants. Antioxidants (and particularly ones that have multiple forms of phenols) are rich sources of plant nutrition that combat oxidative stress in the body that occurs through metabolism, as well as the added stress from toxins that the body must handle. Dark-colored fruits, especially the berries, not only provide ample hydrating water, but also contain lots of polyphenols, a class of foods with nutrients that promote cell health and longevity.

Fruits such as citrus have great amounts of structured water, and lemons and limes help to alkalize the body from their composition. According to Dr. Douillard, extensive studies have indicated that the pith of citrus, with its healthy flavonoid diosmin, has a very favorable impact to foster proper lymph drainage and healthy microcirculation, rather than so many lifestyle choices that are lymph congesting. So when you're eating citrus, make sure you get some of the inner white pith to give your lymph and circulation a natural boost.

Fruit can have a high amount of bioavailable water. Watermelon is up to 92% water and, according to nutritionist Jonny Bowden, does not cause a spike in blood sugar. This popular summer classic is also a rich source of lycopene, a phytonutrient that supports cardiovascular health. Other fruits with water content above 90% are cantaloupe and strawberries. In the 80% range are apples, apricots, brain-boosting blueberries, pineapple, pears, oranges, cherries, grapes and raspberries. Even bananas, full of fiber and potassium, have 74% water. What wonderful ways to boost your water intake!

Even the common carrot has up to 88% water to offer the body along with one of the highest percentages of carotene in a vegetable. The carotene is converted into Vitamin A by the body. This little root vegetable is a virtual nutritional gold mine—chock-full of vitamins, with added minerals potassium, copper and magnesium, as well as other phenolic compounds that promote proper function in the body. For all its fiber density, beets are full of water, minerals and plant pigments that promote healthy function. Other healthy water-laden vegetables include celery, lettuce and the potent detoxifier, the fiery radish. The ever-popular tomato is more than 90% water and a good source of silica.

The lowly cabbage is full of fiber to support intestinal function as well as water. Using cabbage, carrots and radishes to make a homemade slaw is a tasty and crunchy way to cleanse, because the vegetables are hydrating and offer the intestines plenty of fiber to sweep out what is being detoxed. These vegetables also offer a wide array of plant compounds to nourish the body. A light dressing with lemon added brings another detoxifying and alkalizing element to support body function with tastes that are crunchy and filling. I've made this recipe without the standard mayonnaise, simply adding a bit of olive oil with the lemon, some chopped parsley and sea salt. Let it marinate for several hours to let the flavors mingle. Yum.

Other healthy water-filled vegetables include zucchini, bell peppers, spinach, green peas, eggplant, and cruciferous broccoli and cauliflower. Even when cooked, they still can retain a higher volume of water than many other foods that we tend to eat, and the body uses less water to process these. Because water promotes a sensation of fullness, eating water-rich foods allows us to fill up on substances that will restore more function without overeating.

We acknowledge that about everyone needs to watch their intake of sugar, so upping your intake of fruits needs to be balanced. If need be, you can have fruit with cheese, as is the French custom, to add a protein. Fruit with a good bit of fiber does not tend to spike the blood sugar as much as fruit with more juice that is naturally sweet. Adding more fruits and vegetables, with their structured water and easily available nutrients, is simple, since they don't need much preparation—just a little planning ahead to keep some on hand. Chewing on real food like carrot sticks, also known as 'rabbit food' in some circles, can be a simple way to help hydrate, bring in valuable positive plant compounds to promote health and increase the level of fiber, a workhorse in the system. While I had to apply some discipline for a while, I now have a daily urge for my hydrating foods. I really feel better after eating my raw veggies. I'm enjoying that they have a satisfying crunch while bringing precious water into my system.

Another great benefit of plants is that they provide much-needed soluble fiber. This fiber is key for the body to do its work. It absorbs toxins and helps to move them out, and some forms of it are good to build the friendly bacteria that are the flora community in the intestines. Fiber is our friend. It is an effective way that the body binds toxic substances to carry them out of the body and keep them from recirculating and polluting our inner environment.

The body can easily recognize real food at a molecular level. Industrial food making can alter the composition of food so that it is not very recognizable on the micro level, and the body has to expend much-needed resources to digest substances that are marginally useful. This trend is not the right direction for health or longevity.

Eating well by eating what is known as 'real food' is a fast-growing movement in the U.S. for good reason. We need to take back our health and, with it, the ability to creatively engage with life in ways that are empowering and fulfilling. By eating real, tasty and healthy food, we are giving our inundated lymph system a break from the barrage of toxins, as well as providing much-needed nourishment so that it can function in a vital manner. This is clearly a more enjoyable way to have a well-lived life.

Take a Step

As a health educator and ongoing experimenter with food and health, I've found that one of the best ways to make a difference is to make a choice of one new protocol to follow and see how it feels, as part of an ongoing course correction. One thing is usually not too overwhelming, and it's easier to feel like you're doing something and getting a result. This then builds the confidence to continue the discovery process. As we make even small changes, we can begin to get a sense of what it is like to feel better and more confident. This is a great way to overcome resistance. It's really a matter of increasing our awareness and allowing ourselves to explore and discover. Because we have to eat, learning more about what is behind our food choices (both our psychology and habits), can help us have a better perspective about eating and making healthy choices.

In your own daily practice, substitute one old processed or fast food item for one of the better choices when hunger or thirst strikes. Planning ahead is key to have things in the refrigerator and pantry and carried with you throughout the day. The body will thank you for bringing it more nutrients and providing pure water to do its robust work of keeping you healthy!

It can take up to a couple of months to change how our taste buds register different food, especially if we have been used to foods that stir up the adrenal function, giving a quick spike with a drop that follows. This is addictive eating, so it can take a while to adjust, but the body will keep giving good feedback along the way, as it is able to clear and perform its work more easily.

Seeing Red in a Good Way

Choosing food that has a certain level of intact nutrients can make a big difference in how well our lymph can perform all its key roles for the body. Ayurvedic specialist Dr. Douillard suggests eating red foods, with beets as his top choice to improve lymph movement. One of the reasons that beets top his list is they help to cleanse the body in a number of ways. One of the places in the body where the lymph is very interconnected is in the GI tract. Beets are great scrubbers. The fiber in beets is particularly good at clearing substances that have gotten stuck to the villi in the intestines. These tiny threadlike projections in the small intestine can't do their work to absorb nutrients very well if they are not upright and free to move.

The work of beets to act as scrubbers helps the intestines to better absorb fatty acids. Once they are absorbed through the working villi, then the gut lymph known as the lacteals begins the work to transport fatty acids to the venous blood system, where they will eventually be delivered to the liver to complete the metabolizing process. As part of the commitment to health, eating prebiotics and taking probiotics to feed the flora, the good bacterial communities that line the GI tract, is also important to keeping the villi in good shape.

Another highly beneficial aspect of beets is their rich supply of a special form of antioxidants known as betalains. These antioxidants support Phase 2 detox in the body, a vital aspect to help the body rid itself of toxins—and one that is often not functioning optimally. If the body does not have enough nutrients to conjugate the toxins in this phase, they will be re-circulated. Beets provide a bridge to allow the process of detox to be completed so that toxins don't stay inside the body and continue to create a load on the inner system, especially the lymph.

This great root vegetable is also able to thin the bile, a secretion that circulates to help the body digest substances. Because the bile has a major role to regulate the movement of stool and to break down both good and bad fats, it has a lot to handle, and beets help the bile to be the right consistency to do its work well.

Other lymph-supportive red foods include the ever-popular berries, including cranberries. Other deep red treasures include pomegranates and cherries. Writer and holistic nutrition expert Ann Louise Gittleman has recommended pure cranberry juice be added to water to clear the lymph system effectively, because the cranberry is able to emulsify fats, leading to more complete digestion of these large molecules that are carried through the lymph fluids.

To Health, Those Colorful Flavonoids

There have been exciting developments in research about plant compounds happening in the past two decades. Every year now, new information is coming forth about plant chemicals that have very potent antioxidant effects. Flavonoids are colorful compounds that belong to a class of plant phytochemicals known as polyphenols, sources of micronutrients that promote health. Dr. Laurie Barclay has referred to polyphenols as "healing compounds from nature's pharmacy."

Flavonoids are a potent form of phytonutrient found in foods with rich-colored plant pigments. Thus far, over 6,000 forms of these high-nutrient, color-infused chemicals have been identified. Some of the most widely known flavonoids are the beneficial catechins found in green tea. Flavonoids have the ability to counter the destructive effects of free-roaming electrons and even act as catalysts to switch genes on or off. For example, foods that are high in flavonoids are actually able to influence expression of genes in our favor, as they turn on tumor suppressor genes in the body.

Dr. Nalini Chilkov is an integrative medicine doctor who works with patients to help them foster a healthy inner terrain. When this happens, the body is far more capable of defending itself against foreign agents, as well as checking growth of tumors.

Dr. Chilkov wrote, "Cancer is a disease characterized by increased inflammation and oxidative stress from roaming electrons, which damage your DNA the way rust damages metal." The good news is that there is much research being done now into the beneficial effects of chemicals formed from living plants, and one prime example is the anti-inflammatory effect that plants with flavonoids have within our bodies. Flavonoids help tissue systems in the body become more functional again. This is very supportive of the lymph nodes and vessels, whose work puts them in direct contact with oxidative stressors.

According to the Linus Pauling Institute, an even greater effect of flavonoids may be their ability to impact gene expression to properly regulate cell processes in the body through their work to modulate "cell-signaling pathways." These are very lymph-friendly plant pigments, since the purpose of the lymph's work to bathe the cells with fluids is to keep the cells healthy and self-regulating.

Research on plants has been revealing some good news about the apple. It appears that the old adage "an apple a day will keep the doctor away" may have some truth, since studies have linked the good chemicals in apples with a reduced risk of tumor development. Dr. Chilkov heartily endorses the use of apples and other fruits and vegetables that can fortify the body with flavonoids. In apples, for instance, these effects are due to a particular form of flavonoid called quercetin, the most widespread of these types of compounds, found in foods like red onions, cranberries and pomegranates.

Research is also indicating that quercetin has the ability to inhibit the development of cancer cells within the body. This is only one of the many benefits of the more than thirty that have been identified so far for this one flavonoid. Dr. Chilkov mentions one caveat: the intestines have to be healthy enough to absorb quercetin for a good effect, so it is important to make sure the body has enough friendly flora in the GI tract and that the villi are clear and pliable to do their work. This is a very important point—our digestive system needs to be able to absorb and utilize all the good food we take in.

Many foods considered healthy have various forms of flavonoids. Understanding the ability of flavonoids to promote health is one area of very positive development and underscores the point that eating organic, fresh food from plants is a very accessible way to take care of ourselves. It can make the difference between feeling energetic and healthy or exhausted and focused on body issues. Real food makes a big difference in the quality of life.

In addition to the four flavonoid-rich foods named thus far, others include berries, such as blueberries, raspberries and strawberries, and in the citrus family, orange, lemon and grapefruit. Other flavonoid-rich fruits are grapes, cherries, peaches, pears, plums, cantaloupe and watermelon. Now ubiquitous in their usage, tomatoes are officially a fruit, although we treat them as a vegetable. In any case they have a good portion of flavonoids to offer. Among vegetables, we have bell peppers, celery, kale and romaine lettuce, turnip greens, sweet potatoes and cabbage. Almonds are a good source, and the popular pseudo-grain that is actually a seed, quinoa, offers flavonoids for the body to make good use of. Finally, for a little spice, flavonoids are found in hot peppers, including chilis, and the herbs parsley, chamomile and thyme.

More than thirty years ago, Dr. Cousens wrote a groundbreaking book about the 'rainbow' diet suggesting that we include a wide array of colors in making our food choices. At the time it seemed quite out-of-the-box. Now studies on plants are confirming Dr. Cousens' pioneering work to highlight these real foods with deep hues and the importance of making a place for them to foster greater vitality. More recently, another medical doctor has confirmed the value of colorful foods. Dr. Stanley Rockson, a Stanford cardiology and lymph specialist, has identified that flavonoids have an augmenting effect on lymph function. Now that is good news since there are so many tasty flavonoid-rich foods to choose from.

Learning more about how these favorable compounds can benefit us is worth the investment. These foods come with a side benefit of being nutritious and delicious. Flavonoids are but one important kind of plant compound that is proving to be a nutritional powerhouse. The plant world has a wealth of ways to contribute to our health and well-being, so let us make our world richer with the gifts they have to offer. To prove this point, recently Dr. Mark Hyman has written that there are over 25,000 known beneficial chemicals available in colorful vegetables. There is indeed, a medicinal rainbow available in food. Now that's something to chew on.

Juicing for Vitality

A juicing and sprout use advocate known as Sproutman, Steve Meyerowitz, has called juice "plant medicine." Juicing is a way to rapidly saturate the body with living plant nutrients, including much-needed enzymes, vitamins and minerals. Used well, it has the potential to infuse the body with plant elixirs that can quickly bathe the cells in vital compounds such as polyphenols and other antioxidants to both detoxify and rejuvenate the body. Because juice is a highly liquid solution, it serves one of the most important needs of the body: helping it to stay hydrated. Juicing is one of the best ways to boost the body's ability to take in nutrients and detox at the cellular level.

Indeed, as touched on earlier, plants hold their water in ways that are highly bioavailable to our cells when we use them, so it also simplifies the process of receiving nutrition at the micro level, in contrast to much of the food choices of modern fast-paced living that relies heavily on processed foods.

Internal chemistry is also important, and juices, especially citrus, vegetable and green juices, help to alkalize the body and offer minerals to counterbalance the toxic intake of heavy metals and polluting substances that make the body more acidic and therefore more prone to conditions as the body systems degenerate. Celery juice is a marvelous tonic that offers the body a plant-based mineral, sodium, to help the body maintain its inner ocean environment with the right elements. While the sodium in processed and denatured salt is restricted for many related to blood pressure and heart issues, it should not be forgotten that the body's fluids need to have sodium, an alkaline mineral, in the right proportions to maintain balanced hydration internally.

Juices can provide a much-needed infusion of readily absorbable minerals and other nutrients that are not as available in our foods as they were in the past, because of changes in soil chemistry from industrial agriculture. By breaking the cell walls in the process of juicing, the liquid infusion of juice jumpstarts the body with easily absorbable, concentrated nutrition.

Juicing provides major assistance for the body to catch up on dealing with the toxic load it is carrying, since it does not have to expend considerable time to digest juiced fruits and vegetables.

While genes have been considered a key aspect of how long we usually live, modern researchers are beginning to realize that the inner terrain of our bodies has a big impact on how the genes express, for good or ill. Providing our bodies with the right balance of fluid will not only keep it hydrated, but it will also provide much-needed nutrients to nourish the cells. It will give a boost for longevity by supporting the lymph system with living structured fluid that is generally alkaline and easily absorbable.

Known as the 'Juice Lady' from her line of juicing and health books, Bastyr University-trained nutritionist Cherie Calbom has suggested specific vegetables that provide direct assistance to the lymph in detoxing. She recommends cucumbers, parsley, beets, carrots, cabbage and celery to help the body cleanse both the lymph and liver. These two systems are quite interrelated, so it's a good way to let the plant world give a boost internally.

To treat congested lymph that is causing buildup in the nodes or ducts leading to edema in the surrounding tissues, Calbom suggests using one-half of a beet, an apple, one pear, two carrots and two sticks of celery. This six-ounce glass of juice will help to decongest stagnant lymph tissue and drain fluids that have become blocked.

While we may be initially reticent to try different combinations when we begin juicing, it's a very forgiving and enjoyable way to foster health. So far, I've never made a juice I couldn't drink. Even better, I've found lots of new combinations that swirled luscious tastes around my tongue! So play and give your body more nutrition with far less work needed to digest. Below are some of the mainstays of juicing to mix and match and enjoy while improving circulation of the lymph and other interrelated body systems.

Apples add a good touch of sweetness to green drinks, and they have a large number of plant compounds to foster health in the body —juicing makes these very readily absorbable. Quercetin is a very valuable flavonoid in apples.

Beets are good for improving overall circulation, supporting the blood and lymph and detoxing the body.

Carrots have the ability to bolster the immune system, because they help to stimulate white blood cells. This common root is a nutrient-dense plant powerhouse that will support the body's ability to function at a higher level. Carrot juice is a diuretic, so it will also help the body to eliminate excess water. This is good since balancing the level of fluids is a key job of the lymphatic system. This bright vegetable filled with carotenoid also helps to lower stress.

Celery has sodium that helps the cells to maintain the right fluid balance, very key to their proper function. And since maintaining the right fluid balance in the body is a key job for the lymph system, if the cells are able to maintain their fluid balance, it is less work for the lymph.

Citrus is full of structured water, so these fruits help the lymph to have the right internal volume. In addition, this fruit is a powerful internal cleanser that works to keep the lymph working well. Citrus fruit is full of vitamin C to boost immune function.

Leafy greens provide the cleansing power of chlorophyll to the blood and, from there, to alkalize the lymph fluids. Greens are good for the liver and gall bladder to keep them functioning well and carrying out their digestive and detoxing work. Greens that are rich in alkaline minerals (such as magnesium and calcium) are good for both the blood and lymph vessels, helping them to relax and open, thereby countering the restricting effects of stress and acidosis. Lettuce greens are naturally calming. Dandelion greens support the spleen, a major organ of the lymph system, as well as the liver, in its major role to detox as well as coordinating hundreds of body functions. Adding some leafy green herbs to the mix can bring potent antioxidants and aromatics, such as with basil or Thai basil. Parsley is a diuretic that is very detoxing. With herbs, add a small amount to start so the taste is not overwhelming. Greens support health and the right defense operation within.

Ginger is a great root to use in juices because it helps to boost digestive fire, helping the body in its work to break down and process food and not leave undigested food in the blood that becomes internal waste to clear. It also boosts circulation in the body.

Pineapple contains bromelain enzymes that are very effective in breaking down large protein molecules that the lymph transports.

In addition to the juicy plants mentioned above that are mainstays, adding any highly hydrating vegetables such as cucumber or zucchini will give your body a lift in function from being hydrated with living food. Juicing is an energizing, cleansing and very enjoyable mix.

Improving Lymph Function with Enzymes, Herbs, Spices and Other Nutrients

Enzymes

Enzymes are actually protein substances used throughout the body to catalyze every function that keeps us alive. They are very important! Since most of us eat food that is cooked, we use up a lot of the body's enzyme resources within to process the cooked foods being eaten that don't have living enzymes intact. As we age, the production of the body's enzymes tends to dwindle, and these enzymes aren't just used for digesting food but a multitude of metabolic processes that rely on enzymes, including the detoxing work of the lymph and other systems. Enzymes are metabolic keys to life and health because they help the body to regulate every function. As an example, our body's macrophage defenses use proteolytic enzymes to do their work of digesting foreign substances, so the supply of these enzymes is absolutely critical to health.

Because the lymph system is highly challenged by modern-day living, supplementing with enzymes is a way to offer a boost to body systems—and particularly the lymph, because of its critical role in transporting metabolic waste from the body. With less undigested waste in the tissues, the load that the lymph has to transport is lessened. Acidic waste can give rise to opportunistic microbial growth, so it is best not to have this remain in the body. Effectively clearing acidic waste also helps the lymph fluid to remain in the alkaline pH range as it is supposed to be.

Nutrition expert and supplement formulator Jon Barron recommends use of enzymes to counteract the depletion of enzymes from the body through eating mostly cooked food and making poor food choices. He is not alone. Enzymes are powerhouses with catalytic abilities to make much-needed nutrients more available in the body and break down substances so the body can process them more effectively.

In addition to using enzymes with meals, proteolytic enzymes can be used between meals to help the body in its work to clear undigested forms of protein. Many proteins are rather large and these enzymes can help the body to break them down properly so they can be better utilized rather than clogging the lymph system. Use of enzymes can take some burden off the lymph system through lessening undigested food that can become a burden of waste and lead to immune dysfunction.

A good formulation that I have had success with is the line developed by Lou Corona, a raw food advocate and educator for three decades. His line of enzymes is known as the Puradyme Liyfzymes. One of the reasons to recommend it is that the papain in this formula is sulfite-free. As someone who is sulfite-sensitive, it works well for my system. Papain is helpful to unstick the intestinal villa, the tiny workhorses that have a role to absorb food. They also offer a cell regenerator antioxidant enzyme formula. Use of this kind of formula can give the body a big boost in clearing out undigested substances and waste from unfriendly microbe colonies that can take a big toll on body function.

Having worked with enzymes for years, I know first hand how they can make a big difference in how well the body functions and how good you feel daily. With the increasing number of ways that we are exposed to toxins from food and products and the effects of stress from our fast pace of life itself, one of the simplest methods to give the body a healthy boost is to add a broad-spectrum quality enzyme and notice if there is a difference in function. Like all supplements, it's best to buy one that is plant-based and pure as possible, without fillers.

Another way to make it easier on the body to process food is to eat in smaller portions throughout the day and to give the body more delicious, nutrient-dense options when you do eat. Nutrient dense food will take longer to break down and leave more of a feeling of fullness and satisfaction from ingesting real food. Making a habit of drinking water sometimes when there is an urge to eat adds to a feeling of fullness that is healthy and hydrating.

Herbs and Spices

Use of herbs and spices is a very simple and effective means to improve the body's ability to detox. Because our lifestyle tends to create sluggish lymph, Dr. Lemole suggests herbs to help dilate the lymph vessels and unblock where external toxins and unprocessed foodstuffs have hindered the vital cleansing and balancing work of the lymph. Dr. Lemole's primary recommendation for an unclogging herb is red clover, made into a tea or taken as a capsule. Not only does this herb provide antioxidant nutrition for better lymph function, it helps out two of the body's other key detox systems, as well—the liver and the kidneys.

Echinacea and astragalus are two well known immune strengtheners that can lower inflammation in the body and help to alleviate lymph stagnation. They are readily available as tinctures, capsules or teas. Echinacea helps both the lymphocytes and macrophages to do their work better. Because stress has been indicated as a strong contributor to congestion of the lymph system, an adaptogenic herb like astragalus is good because it increases the body's capacity to be more resilient and adaptive to daily stressors.

Another herb with a long history of usage for healing purposes is burdock. Burdock root, a staple in macrobiotic food, is quite earthy and tasty when used in rice or veggie combinations. In macrobiotic diets burdock is used to return the body to more healthy balance, and it is effective in promoting lymph movement, as well as bile, a secretion that is key in healthy function. It can be used as a tea, and it is also available as a tincture that can be diluted in water.

A plant known as 'red root,' a member of the Ceanothus family (*Ceanothus americanus*), is recommended to help get stagnant lymph moving. Herbalist Michael Moore suggests it is also useful to address portal venous stagnation, because it corresponds with stagnation of the lymph. Because portal blood does not have its own pressure and has to flow upward to the liver, it is more prone to sluggish conditions. He makes a tea with this herb. "The dose for the tea is small, however, from one-eighth to one-quarter cup of a standard decoction."

Dr. Douillard praises another premier red root, known as manjistha in Ayurveda, for its ability to decongest the lymph, purify the blood and fortify the liver with its antioxidant capacity. These systems are all key for health and proper detox, so this is quite a potent herb. Its amazing ability does not stop here. It is also able to keep fats in the lymph and the liver from becoming bad fats. This is a very remarkable contribution to the body. The proper name of manjistha is *Rubia cordifolia*. It is also called Indian madder root. This vining plant is used to balance the blood and to address skin issues as part of its beneficial influence on the body.

Another earthy-colored herb that helps clear congested lymph is sarsaparilla. The plant compound known as saponins works in the body to reduce the load of non-beneficial microbes and clear away toxins. Sarsaparilla is also good for cleansing the blood and the lymph.

Garlic stimulates lymph function, so let it flavor your food and get a good boost on detoxing. Other herbs that can stimulate good lymph function include dandelion root.

Another lesser-known herb that is effective in supporting lymph function is *Centella asiatica*, known in Ayurveda as brahmi. According to Dr. Douillard, this herb increases microcirculation that is key to balancing congested lymph and supporting proper detox in the body. By improving movement at the cellular level, it improves nutrient inflow to the cells and therefore increases the body's ability to restore health more readily. As an effective catalyst to counter stress, this herb is a very lymph-friendly plant.

The plant world has an abundance of offerings to assist the right inner environment, and one that is not commonly thought of is ginkgo biloba, one of the oldest plants on the planet. It has a healthy supply of flavonoids that are basically plant antioxidants. This plant and the well known Asian panacea, ginseng, are two that can help to increase aerobic metabolism internally, a function that definitely needs augmenting among a population that is very sedentary.

Turmeric is an important spice for increasing circulation, supporting the detox function of the liver, and increasing the body's antioxidant levels. As if that were not enough, this earthy root stimulates metabolism and catalyzes the body to offload unfavorable internal freeloaders. With the onslaught of toxins that our bodies are bombarded by, turmeric is a wonder spice, because it helps the cell to maintain its integrity. No wonder that this golden-hued root has been a staple in India for thousands of years.

Several other fiery spices can help to dilate vessels and stimulate circulation so that the blood system is more efficient in handling nutrients and waste, thereby lessening the load of inner debris that the lymph must transport. These spices include cayenne, ginger and horseradish. While for some they are an acquired taste, a little bit will help to increase circulation internally that can help to counter the effects of sluggish conditions within, especially constricted vessels of the lymph or blood.

Dr. Sears highly recommends the use of herbs and spices in his practice. It's inspiring that he walks the talk in his own diet and offers up some of his best suggestions for improving health at home. (See the Resources section for some formulas with lymph- boosting and draining herbs.)

Because it is all too common for a sedentary lifestyle combined with poor food choices and eating habits to created clogged lymph, the effort that it takes to make a shift will be rewarded with better functioning body systems overall. The lymph is a major detox system that is too often clogged, so it can become too viscous from acid waste that isn't moving quickly enough.

One of the best things we can do to champion our own longevity is to take simple steps to course-correct how we are aligning with our lymph system. Where there are blockages, herbs and spices can be both enjoyable and effective ways to help the body's lymph system to open up and clear waste. Enzymes can help to break down incompletely processed protein and fat throughout the body, improving the functioning of the lymph fluids and nodes to act as they are designed to, as efficient cleansers and filters.

Other nutrients to support lymph function

To help cleanse and strengthen, the B vitamins improve the functional efficiency of the lymph and are key factors to activate enzymes needed for healing. Vitamin A is good for all tissues in the body, including the lymph tissue, such as in nodes and vessels. Zinc is an important mineral for the body's immune function. It helps the white blood cells circulating in the lymph to function better and reduce lymph congestion.

A supplement that is recommended by cardiologist and lymph expert Dr. Lemole is CoQ10. He recommends it because he has found that, especially after age fifty, the supply of CoQ10 in the body is usually quite low. CoQ10 is a compound that is used by the body's cells in the process of metabolism, so it is a critical substance for good function.

A CoQ10 product by Garden of Life essentially serves a two-fold role for the body because it provides this much-needed antioxidant compound along with a high proportion of omega-3 oil, and lesser amounts of 6 and 9. Since the lymph system is the primary transport for large oil molecules that we eat in food, it is best that we find a better balance with the kind and quantity of oils that we take in, so that the lymph system is not so challenged or compromised.

According to raw food expert Victoria Boutenko, some of the best proportions of omega-3 fatty acids that we can ingest come from flax oil, flax seeds, chia, green lettuce and spinach. With strawberries and bananas, the omega-6s are a little higher, but they are still in a good proportion.

The mineral magnesium, as mentioned earlier, is often quite deficient in the standard diet. Many green foods are a good source of it, yet green is not our favorite color of food to ingest. The 'whites' are much more preferred, as in French fries, pizza and other flour products and sugared sweets with bleached cane sweetener.

The vital alkalizing and relaxing mineral magnesium is used in over 300 body functions, so we need more greens as one way to up the intake. More nutritionists are revising their recommendations to increase magnesium intake, even to double that of calcium intake. As with all supplements and foods, it's best to pay attention to your body's feedback, notice whether something is working well or not and gradually increase when starting a new regime so you can tell what is happening and buffer possible healing reactions.

Magnesium is also abundant in foods other than leafy greens, namely the ever-popular banana, as well as the seed quinoa, which has a whopping 118 milligrams of magnesium per half-cup serving. The seeds of sunflower, pumpkin, hemp and chia are also good sources. In the nut family, good levels of magnesium are found in cashews and almonds. In the grains, both oatmeal and rice provide good sources. In the legume family, lentils, black beans and kidney beans are rich sources of this important mineral.

So you can obtain abundant magnesium from a variety of foods, not to mention the water-grown algae forms, spirulina and chlorella. Magnesium is the ultimate anti-stress mineral, and in our world of multitasking and sensory bombardment, it is needed in greater quantities to buffer the effects of overstimulation and to keep the body healthy. It is especially helpful for vessels, to help them relax from stress-induced constriction.

Dr. Douillard recommends the trace mineral iodine as an effective lymph mover. He has indicated that iodine deficiency is a major reason that lymph isn't functioning to detox as it is designed. With the right absorption of iodine in the diet, it will resolve lymphatic congestion as well as improve its ability to eliminate toxins from the body as well. Dr. Cousens has a good bit to say about the importance of this metabolizing mineral, how deficient it is in most modern diets and how important it is to help the body detox and keep its defenses in prime condition.

Sea vegetables are another good way to help the body detox, largely due to their mineral content. These sea wonders are also good lymph supporters because they help the body to let go of fluid buildup in the body, so this ocean 'produce' is a natural support for better lymph function. The lymph system is the body's built-in backup for vascular fluid leakage that happens all the time. Up to 10-20% of the blood plasma is not immediately absorbed back into the arterial capillaries, and the lymph is the designated 'driver' to transport this fluid back to the venous system.

Some forms of sea vegetables are also good sources of the mineral iodine discussed above. Sea vegetables include the algae forms chlorella and spirulina, as well as seaweeds and other saline-growing vegetables, such as laver. Consider adding wakame, kelp, nori or dulse to dishes such as cooked beans (good with aduki beans especially), soups and even salads. (See the Resources section for the Chickpea and Sea Veggie Salad recipe.) Check where this sea produce is grown, though, since many ocean zones are now highly polluted. Spirulina is one algae that is grown in alkaline ponds, so it is easier to maintain purity than in some ocean areas. Buying from a company with documented high standards is the best bet.

Soil content will always determine how much any food can be a carrier of a mineral. Foods that tend to be high in iodine include: blueberries, carrots, cucumbers, garlic, onions, eggplant, leaf lettuce, green peppers, kale, oats, potatoes, spinach, squash, strawberries, tomatoes and watermelon.

Some of the other major alkalizing minerals that should be incorporated into our diet to maintain the body's equilibrium are calcium, potassium and sodium. Lemons are a good source of three of the major alkalizing minerals: magnesium, calcium and potassium. It's no surprise then that they are such a wonder fruit to assist the body. Other minerals needed in lesser amounts are iron, zinc, manganese, boron and nickel. Remember we need some of the acid minerals, and a notable one for lymph health is iodine. The issue with our daily diet is that we're either facing general mineral deficiency based on what is not in the soil or is lacking in a diet of processed foods. Minerals are too often overlooked as part of health and maintaining the right inner chemistry for our blood plasma and lymph fluids to function properly.

For the lymph to do its work properly to detox, the right minerals must exist in the fluid medium itself. Sodium chloride, bicarbonate, along with some potassium and calcium are needed in the proper amounts for the blood and lymph systems. Oriental Medicine Doctor Michael Tierra has spoken to how the right proportions of sodium and potassium in solution are key to promoting exchanges between the inside and outside of the cell. In the right proportions, there is an "electrical charge that helps in carrying food, fluid and waste into and out of the cells." Potassium is in higher concentration inside the cell and sodium is more concentrated in the extracellular fluids. No surprise then that the lymph is a reservoir of the mineral sodium.

Some sodium rich foods include the ever-popular apple, and beets, a mainstay of the healthy lymph diet. Vegetables that are high in sodium are asparagus, cabbage, carrots, okra and celery, kale, collards, dandelion greens, mustard and New Zealand spinach greens especially. In the fruit arena, figs, dates, coconuts, apricots, strawberries and black olives are good sources of sodium. Other food substances with good amounts of sodium include horseradish, sunflower and sesame seeds, lentils, and the sea vegetables kelp, dulse and Irish moss.

Foods high in potassium are the bitter greens with the highest content in watercress. Sea vegetables include dulse, Irish moss and kelp (also good sources of sodium). Black olives that have been sun-dried are also a good source. Beans high in potassium are lentils and white beans. Meat sources include pork. Fish that are potassium-rich include halibut and tuna. Vegetables include broccoli, potatoes, both white and sweet, and squash. Fruits with good proportions of potassium include oranges, bananas and cantaloupe. While milk is known for its calcium, whole milk and yogurt are also good sources of this important mineral as well.

A diet high in fruits and vegetables will provide a healthy dose of antioxidants needed to help the lymph pathways—from its tiny capillaries to its main vessels—counter oxidative effects from direct exposure to toxins. Just think, daily this part of our body is doing its best to mediate toxicity. We need to become much more appreciative and hopefully supportive of this behind the scenes ally. As in the blood circulatory system, these vessels are exposed to wear and tear that can really diminish their ability to function as a major transport system responsible for removing toxins and foreign organisms. A recommendation from naturopathic doctor Lise Alschuler is to use green tea, since it is an abundant source of antioxidants, for healthy lymph function.

An Ounce of Prevention is Worth a Pound of Cure

We are used to thinking that if it's on the shelf or available in the grocery store, we don't have to think about what we eat, put on our skin or use in our household. Unfortunately this is no longer true. Now, thousands upon thousands of chemical substances are put into manufactured products that we can't even pronounce, let alone recognize whether they are safe to use. The problem with lots of them is that our bodies don't recognize them either, and this can lead to an overzealous protective mechanism that can become a chronic autoimmune reaction. Fortunately, many more doctors are recognizing the effects that chemicals can have on people's health and becoming better advocates for more natural methods of maintaining and improving health.

Longevity studies looking at cultures around the world have pointed to some basics to incorporate. One of the key guidelines is to eat a mostly plant-based diet of food with nutrients intact.

One of the best proactive measures anyone can do as a consumer to serve better lymph and immune function is to begin cutting down on products and processed food that are laden with manmade chemicals that burden the body with toxins. Read the label. If it has lots of ingredients with names that are unrecognizable, make another choice. Do your best to cut back on toxic chemical infusions that pollute the vital inner fluid system known as the lymph. Play and be carefree with your intake on occasion, but cut out the daily habit of eating lots of denatured, i.e., processed, foods as the mainstay of your diet if you want to be healthy. Cultivating savvy food habits that are also savory can be an enjoyable way to foster longevity.

[3]
Self-Help Practices

As life continues to move at a faster pace and we are called to adapt more quickly, self-help forms of care are even more important to maintain some balance. Practices that nurture and strengthen so that we can maintain a level of adaptability are key. This section includes some of the best I have found. As with all things in this book, you're encouraged to experiment and find what works best for your healthy lifestyle. Use your discretion in beginning any new lifestyle practices. First, check in with yourself to see if a practice really resonates with your body and life situation. Having worked with healing and holistic health for two decades, I believe that the more we can listen to our own inner messages and guidance, the better off we will be. I find that starting slow and seeing how your body responds is a good way to introduce new practices.

If you have a medical or health condition, it is always wise to talk with your doctor or qualified health practitioner if there is any question or concern to be considered. This information is offered to bring a broader perspective on choices available to live a healthier and happier lifestyle. Choose wisely.

Self-Help Good Lymph Moves

If you want to help your lymph do its very important work of clearing out daily waste, foreign microorganisms and managing the fluid balance in the body, then movement is a vital necessity because the lymph does not have its own heart pump. To give you an idea of the inner housecleaning that needs to happen daily, 500 million cells die and need to be cleared. As you can tell just from this example, lymph fluid circulation is much needed to keep waste moving to the organs of elimination such as the liver, kidneys and skin.

While some of the large vessels have smooth muscle that can contract to help the movement of lymph fluids, the primary way that lymph moves is through a simple design. As we move, our skeletal muscles stimulate the lymph fluids to move. Taking full breaths is another major stimulus to effectively move the lymph fluids.

Anything that improves circulation will support better lymph function, so any aerobic activity is beneficial. Tai chi and qigong are two Eastern mind body practices that will improve energy flow and circulation and thereby boost lymph function.

While strenuous aerobic activity and sports will certainly boost lymph function and circulation, according to Dr. Lemole, "For the purposes of keeping the heart and the lymphatic system healthy, such exercise is not necessary, though it does benefit muscle tone and aids in weight loss."

Aerobic moves not only increase circulatory function that gives a boost to the lymph, it is a way to naturally sweat out toxins and lighten the load that the lymph has to dispose of. So thumbs up on aerobic practices to stay healthy and glowing. While one doesn't have to be an athlete to accomplish much better flow, this note to the coach potatoes among us—you do need to get a move on.

Self-Help Walking

Dr. Lemole believes walking is one of the best exercises for the lymph, and it's an exercise that can be done about anywhere, making it very accessible to engage in. Walking involves the skeletal muscles that are prime movers of lymph fluid so it is great for stimulating lymph function. He recommends a brisk pace for 30 minutes a day. Make sure your arms are moving for the best result. John Ossipinski has a good suggestion; while you're moving, up the pace for a short sprint for about 40 seconds to provide a good effect on the heart. This can help to keep plaque from building up in the arteries by increasing blood flow.

To get the most from your walking lymph stimulation session, use the time to breathe fully. Walking outside is a great time to get out of your head and into the enjoyment of moving in the body, of noticing sensory delights of nature. Could there be a better way of becoming more fully oxygenated? Let your arms swing and develop a cadence with your body and your breath. It's simple and very refreshing. Life is complicated and getting back to the basics of feeling what it's like to just be at home in the body is a daily reminder we can all use.

An inspiration led me to add a bit of lift to my walking regime. I started what I call 'lymph walking' to increase the pump of the movement by lifting onto the front of my foot as I walk. It's playful and acts to boost my spirit as I take some of my walking steps.

A walk can offer a sense of spaciousness to counter the compressed sense of many daily demands. So enjoy some free time to fully exhale and let go, feeling more open and flowing.

Self-Help Get a Jump on It!

Using a rebounder is a perfect option to improve lymph circulation. It gives the body a workout through the up-and-down motion—a great stimulus because the major lymph return channels run vertically up the body into the thoracic area. Through the expansion of going up and being weightless for a second and then coming down as gravity exerts its pull—it exerts G-force momentum to move body fluids, registering all the way down to the cellular level.

Lymph is very slow moving. With twice the volume of the blood plasma, the lymph may drain about 1.5-2 liters of fluid per day. Rebounding is a simple way to get a great boost for cleansing, and it simultaneously helps to build muscle tone and assists with joint mobility. This activity stimulates all the fluid systems in the body, helping the entire system to receive a boost in circulation.

Rebounding is an easy form of exercise that has a very broad and positive effect with little wear and tear on the body. Even people that are very sedentary can gently move on the rebounder to improve the circulation of fluids. Start slow to get things moving because rebounding does promote detox.

Even those that have been sedentary can lightly bounce for a couple of minutes at a time to start, keeping your feet on the rebounder. You can have someone stand with you to stabilize the light movement if you're just checking it out. Being gentle and adding a bit of bounce can improve fluid movement over time. If you have health concerns, check with your doctor or health professional before beginning this kind of regimen to be sure.

If you plan to get vigorous in rebounding, be sure to warm up by bouncing slowly and let your body get going before you move into big bouncing. Then slow back down again as you finish, the same as you would with other forms of exercise.

Bouncing While Standing

Bouncing in place while standing can be done about anywhere. To begin, you just let the body be at ease and bounce lightly up and down for five minutes. With shoulders relaxed and arms at your side, just let the body go up and down in a continuous motion. Be sure to keep breathing smoothly as well. This is very naturally relaxing and easily accessible.

This simple exercise from qigong master Chunyi Lin is a wonderful way to support lymph and digestive tissue function. For an extra boost, he recommends raising your arms overhead and letting the hands drop and bounce for another few minutes. Lightly bouncing with the arms overhead helps not only the lymph, but also the lungs, glands and heart.

According to John Ossipinski, any activity that stretches the arms overhead offers a boost to activate the major return duct (located on the left side). With all the ways that this area can become constricted, it's a good idea to incorporate daily practices to open up the thoracic and chest area. So get to stretching and bouncing!

Jumping for Joy

In our increasingly sedentary world, we can pause for a few moments and do some good old-fashioned jumping jacks. Yes. You can do the jumping for a few minutes between sedentary sessions to keep things moving as it were. The good news is that since you're moving your arms and legs at the same time, it really gives a boost to pump the body's fluids. This is a joyful thing to do, recalling younger years, and may prove not only to be good for the flow, but also to bring an uptick from emotional and mental preoccupations, as you shift away from daily problems for a few minutes. It's definitely a pause that stimulates and can refresh the perspective as well.

Self-Help Lymph Stretches

Specific exercises that support the lymph function by promoting circulation and drainage are included below. This set of stretches was developed at the Ohio State University Comprehensive Cancer Center to address lymphedema after surgery. They are included here because they make an easy set of stretching exercises to promote muscle contraction and movement, since this promotes healthy activation of the lymph.

Love Your Lymph is focused on providing information and self-help lifestyle options to boost general lymph function. Lymphedema is a health condition affecting millions of people. For information on lymphedema as a chronic condition or that is a medical situation, check the Resources section for further reading. Professional treatment is important to foster greater circulation and drainage with the condition of lymphedema. Techniques that are medically appropriate for the condition may be learned from a doctor or professional therapist trained in specific techniques for lymphedema.

If you're short on time, the first four stretches will help have the greatest effect, helping to open the neck into thoracic areas where the major lymph return junctions are under the collarbones.

1. Neck Roll Side-to-Side

Lying flat on a surface, take a breath and, as you exhale, let your head roll to the right as far as it wants to go comfortably. When it stops, then inhale and bring the head back to center. As you begin to exhale, let the head drop to the left as far as it wants to go. Breathe in and come back to center. Repeat 5-10 times. This opens up the neck area where a lot of drainage occurs from sinuses in the head. Most people hold a lot of tension in this part of the body, and this constricts vessel tissue, so use the breath and the force of gravity to allow a gentle opening for more ease.

2. Head Tilt

Slowly move the right side of the head down toward your shoulder as far as it is comfortable. Hold for a few seconds, then easily bring your head back up. Repeat 5-10 times. Repeat the tilt with the left side of the head.

3. Shoulder Roll

Lift your shoulders up and make circles 5-10 times to loosen up this area that is usually held fairly tightly. This should be gentle and easy throughout.

4. Shoulder Shrug

You can do this exercise either standing or sitting. With your spine straight, lift your shoulders up as far as they will comfortably go, hold a second, then let go with a full exhale. This releases tension in the shoulder and upper thoracic area, another place in the body affected by stress, especially the over stimulated fight or flight response from daily challenges. Repeat this 5-10 times, depending on how much tension is being held. The thoracic duct is the largest drain for lymph back into the circulatory system, so this one helps to open up tissue around this area through movement and letting go with the breath.

5. Elbow Bend

Lying flat, raise your elbow toward the shoulder and then bring it down. You can do this in cycle with the breath or not. Repeat 5-10 times. Repeat on the other side.

6. Pelvic Tilt

Lying on a flat surface with the body straight, lift your knees slightly while keeping the feet on the ground about hip-width apart. Using your abdominal muscles, press your lower back down toward the flat surface and hold to a count of ten, then release the contraction and let the body relax for a few moments. Try to do this in a slow, easy rhythm. Repeat up to 10 times.

7. Leg Flexing

Lying flat, easily slide one leg up so the knee is flexed as far as is comfortable, then slowly return it to the floor. Repeat on the other side and do both legs 5-7 times.

8. Ankle Pumps

Lying flat on a surface, begin to flex and extend your ankle. On the inhale flex the ankle, then when you let out the breath, extend it, pointing your toe away from the body. Repeat 6-10 times. Repeat on the other side.

Self-Help Stomach Crunches

Since a majority of the body's lymph nodes are concentrated in the abdomen and the neck, this classic exercise is one recommended by John Ossipinski to have a good activating effect on a large number of nodes as well as creating a stimulating effect on the vessels that run up the front of the body. The recommended exercise is the stomach crunch.

Lay flat on a solid surface with your knees bent with feet flat. Place arms across the chest in a relaxed manner. Once comfortably positioned, then raise your head and shoulders up slightly. Again, do a small number of crunches (5-10) and build up as you gain more strength. Waking up centers that have become sluggish is the goal, so just add in a bit as your capacity builds. When finished, spend a few seconds letting your body relax while doing some full breaths to completely let go of the muscle contraction part of the exercise.

Full Breathing

Our bodies are wonderfully designed systems that perform countless intelligent actions to keep us functioning 24/7. One way that the body essentially steers our vehicle to function optimally is through the breath. From a biological standpoint, the breath is also the source of oxygen, so critical a substance that we can live only minutes without it. In yoga, the breath is the source of prana, a subtle substance that is also needed in order to live.

Most of the time, if we're breathing, we think we're doing all right. Part of the problem is we don't notice that as stressed-out modern-day people, we're taking in less and less oxygen, breathing at the top of our lungs and not using the lungs as the bellows that they are meant to be—a kind of inner pump that enriches the body with much-needed oxygen.

Both the lungs and the diaphragm play a vital role in respiration that becomes more diminished with the cumulative effects of stress. The diaphragm is a thin sheet of muscle shaped like a dome that sits below the lungs and above the abdominal cavity. Unless we're involved in some kind of aerobic activity, it's easy to have the breath become constricted and not really notice the cumulative effect. Take a moment now to check in and see if you're breathing full, belly-deep breaths or if your body is trying to live on short little sniffs of air. Just as important—are you really exhaling? If not, it's an indication that the body is not letting go of stress in the moment. A full inhale and exhale is necessary to nourish the body and is the ultimate in stress relief.

The Breath and Stress

According to Dr. Cousens, "The vast majority of humanity lives in the chemistry of stress." This is expressed as tension in the muscles that can become a mantle of vigilance. Stress sends us into the fight or flight part of the nervous system, and the sympathetic activating system shuts down digestion because it's not critical while we're on alert. Given how much time we spend in this mode, our bodies are not getting much of the green light to digest.

Continued stress brings with it a sense of unease, anxiety and a racing mind that are also symptoms of what he calls an adrenal stress syndrome. Many years ago I was doing session work with a lady who had relocated from New York, her hometown. She had a very shallow breathing pattern that was linked with a lot of nervousness. No wonder. Not only was her body not receiving enough oxygen because of this pattern, it was sending signals of distress to the brain because her body was continually short on oxygen. The situation was difficult because she had lost the connection to the breath as the basic resource in life. Restricted breathing has been linked with more than a majority of the ills to health. It is not only key to staying alive, but to feeling good as well.

Breathing is a basic function of life, so we need to remind ourselves that stress causes a constriction that restricts essential oxygen intake. This can become a self-perpetuating cycle that diminishes body function because restricted oxygen then lessens the viability of the cells, since this nutrient is a vital necessity.

At the micro level, the lymph fluid has a role to carry away debris and gases such as carbon dioxide and nitrogen. When stress causes congestion in the lymph, then the already slow fluid movement can become sluggish. If gases and debris aren't moving out, it essentially pollutes the lymph fluid and causes more inner buildup of waste. If stress has lessened breathing, then this registers in the body as a lower level of oxygen-saturated blood. If this vital nutrient isn't infused in the blood, then it will be deficient in the lymph fluid that bathes the cells as well. When the lymph flows around the cells, it brings nutrients and carries away the used-up metabolites from the cellular activity. If the lymph has not received an appropriate influx of nutrients, including oxygen, then there is not enough to exchange for what has been used up. It's a cycle that diminishes body function while increasing the risk that at some point a deficient condition will become a degenerative one.

Rather than letting stress cause habitual shallow breathing and buildup of toxic waste, the best remedy is to learn how to breathe fully as a way of life, not just during yoga or while walking or running, as good as this is. We need an abundant supply of life energy that comes with the simple action of breathing deeply. With full breathing, the bottom third of the lungs, where there is more blood, can become saturated with life-giving oxygen.

Every cell in our body is dependent on a continuing supply of this element in order to remain alive and healthy. For the lymph system to work well, we need to be proactive in breathing properly. Through full breathing, the lungs exert pressure upon the thoracic duct, the major drainage pathway to return lymph fluids to the venous system. Full breathing is an effective pump to keep the lymph in circulation.

When I was new to bodywork, I was having sessions with a mentor. He remarked on what a good exhale I had. I appreciated his comment because I had worked on not holding my breath, as it were. I had noticed people I was working with were in a kind of 'holding' mode and I had decided that I wanted to get past this pattern myself. It was also around the time that the film *Waiting to Exhale* came out, and I thought that was an apt description of what was happening unconsciously in many lives, including my own.

Stress causes restriction in the tissue. If something causes a disturbance and there is a reaction to stop the complete breath rhythm, one of the best methods that can be employed to remain relatively stress-free is to just take some deep breaths and completely exhale. What an amazing practice to remain conscious and energized.

The breath is our basic resource, and we just need to remember that in the course of daily life, as we feel challenged, stressed or overloaded, to come back to the breath. It brings an immediate opening and expansion to meet life in all its facets. Taking a full breath is one of the simplest methods of releasing tension, while receiving the much-needed nutrient of oxygen-enriched blood.

Self-Help Learning to Breathe Again

A full, deep breath should be a natural way that we interact with the world, but all too often it is not. For this reason, a simple practice of finding a peaceful place to spend a few minutes doing full deep breathing will be a potent resource to restore more balance. This calls upon the calming parasympathetic nervous system to regulate the body's relaxing functions. With a full breath, the belly swells outwardly like a balloon and allows for the vital organs to expand, providing an internal massaging action for the organs. As you begin to be present with your breath, just keep it simple. Inhale to a point where the breath stops and then slowly let it out. As you continue, you may notice that there is a deeper in breath happening, but most importantly, just breath and do as little analyzing as possible.

The healthy effect of a simple, full-belly breath can be heightened with some positive imagery, like looking at something beautiful, or listening to soft music or quietly chanting to direct the mind in a positive direction. This simple practice can be a much-needed mini-retreat to restore a deeper sense of calming resources. YAM is a heart center sound that helps to open up the chest cavity so that it can relax. This simple therapy is instantly effective. It is good for the heart, lungs and lymph system. If you feel called to do it, take in a breath and as you let it out, say Y-A-M slowly on the exhale breath.

Through breathing in a full and complete manner, we not only oxygenate the body, this kind of breathing creates a form of pressure pumping within to help push the lymph up the front lymph channels that are the ducts where lymph returns to blood circulation.

The body is designed to create health with thousands of interactions occurring in the moment. We just need to get onboard to support our body's function in some basic ways to reap a harvest of benefits from the intelligence already programmed into our system.

Self-Help Horizontal Health Squat

Waste gas is not meant to be stored in the tissues for any length of time. This protocol will help the body to release trapped gases and other waste in the body and thereby decrease the burden of toxins being stored by stimulating a downward flow of energy. This pose, known as a horizontal squat, also helps to restore inner equilibrium and effectively brings relief from stress and tension. The squat is soothing and relaxing.

Lie flat on a comfortable solid surface, and draw your knees up and let them rest into the body. Relax as much as you can while wrapping your arms around your legs. Hold for 3-5 minutes for a good effect internally. You can also slowly rock side-to-side as well. Don't forget to do some full breathing while in the pose to increase the positive momentum.

A vertical health squat is more effective, but unless you're active physically and used to stretching, the lying down version is much safer, so it is recommended here. The vertical squat is Dr. Stone's favorite health boosting posture. The squat is a pose that helps the body to eliminate all forms of waste stored within, and restore more balance and energy flow. The squat not only helps with the right downward flow, used consistently, it will help the body to be more vital. It's such a simple and very effective practice to balance on many levels. If interested in learning more about Dr. Stone's squat, you can check it out on the site http://www.digitaldrstone.org.

A note here: carbon dioxide is a substance that we release after the body does its work, so taking in carbonated drinks with this gas in it is counter to our natural cycle. Plants give us oxygen and use carbon dioxide. Dr. Stone believed that oxygen was restricted from being absorbed in the tissues and cells because of waste gases such as carbon dioxide that were stored in the body and not being eliminated effectively. This protocol helps the lymph by giving energetic impetus for the body to be more effective in letting go of waste that the lymph transports as part of its load. It is mentioned here to bring attention to the need to do our best to avoid doing things that are quite contrary to our design if we want to live long *and* well.

Yoga

The mind-body practice of yoga—basically doing asana or posture practice—has mushroomed in the last fifteen years. Yoga brings a great benefit to increase inner circulation, restores proper breathing function and frees up tissues throughout the body that have become tight and compressed. Yoga exerts a restorative influence to the body's organs, down to the cells, through twists, inversions and yogic breath practices.

The practice of postures exerts a positive influence on the lymphatics. According to yoga convert Dr. Lemole, "It relaxes the lymph channels and dramatically increases lymph flow through muscular and gravitational pumping of the lymphatic system." He also writes that when a yoga practice involves positive and peaceful images, it stimulates hormonal messengers and creates an opening and relaxing of lymphatic channels. This allows much-needed drainage to occur, helping the body release toxins from the nodes and other body tissues. This is a great confirmation of mind body unity. We can apply this not only with yoga, but with any of our nourishing and restorative practices, like meditation, qigong, or simple breathing, to boost the function of the lymph.

Because most people learn yoga postures by going to a studio, they will not be covered here. Some forms of yoga are more intensive with poses that squeeze and contract muscles and this brings a benefit. Softer forms, such as vinyasa, focuses on the yoga of flow and we know that this is a very important quality for the fluid lymph system. 'Hot' yoga is great not only for pose stimulating lymph movement, it provides a major detox through sweating, effectively lowering the level of internal toxins that the lymph system has to transport.

Lymphatic Yoga

A longtime yoga teacher and student of the lymphatic system, Edely Wallace has developed a new form of yoga practice that is quite germane to our focus on the lymph. She has studied the lymph system for more than two decades, and is a certified lymph therapist. As a yoga student and now teacher for over thirty years, she brings an unusual breadth of knowledge to her work. Appropriately called lymphatic yoga, Wallace has developed a yoga set of twenty-three postures to tune up lymph function and maintain this vital fluid system.

From her perspective these lymphatic yoga postures will have the best effect on the lymph. The next best option she recommends is to do full diaphragmatic breathing while walking. Third best is swimming. Swimming can be a kind of mindful meditation, as it requires a complete breath as an automatic part of the exercise. (For more, see the Resources section.)

Pranayama

Many people primarily think of yoga as a set of postures, yet in the East, where this mind body system originated, this rich lineage has many facets. One of them is known as pranayama. This Sanskrit word refers to practices that teach about how to control the breath. Pranayama is a key facet of yoga that can make a huge difference not just in how we breathe, but in how we perceive our lives. As we've seen, proper breathing is part of our inherent design, a kind of organic fuel to catalyze optimal function within the body system, bringing in much-needed oxygen.

Practicing pranayama can provide the massage of tissue systems and stoke the inner chemistry to increase the life force. In this field of study, yogis are focusing on integrating the subtle essence within the breath, the prana, to vitalize on all levels—physical, emotional and mental. Breathing is such a developed spiritual art form that it can be used to stimulate much higher states of well-being and awareness. Yogic breath techniques are very effective in moving beyond sluggish states of the mind and emotions, as well as in the body.

Mudras

Another form of yoga that is not yet widely practiced in the West, but is very accessible to people of all ages and stages of health is known as doing mudras. This is yoga using the hands. While it might seem like it couldn't do much, it is really quite powerful. It's a great way to turn the dial on energies—down when there are symptoms of discomfort from an unbalanced condition, or up if more vitality is needed.

Mudras can have a good effect where there is congestion or sluggishness. Rather than having to find a yoga studio or special spot to practice, they can even be done while standing in line at the bank, watching television or resting. Several mudras are included below to help shift energy and assist the lymph and other fluids in the body to have greater movement. Doing mudras can become a daily practice to easily course correct energy flow.

Self-Help Breath and Mudras

Here's one example of a practice that can help to open up the breath, one of the most important catalysts for proper lymph circulation.

Self-Help Diaphragmatic Breathing

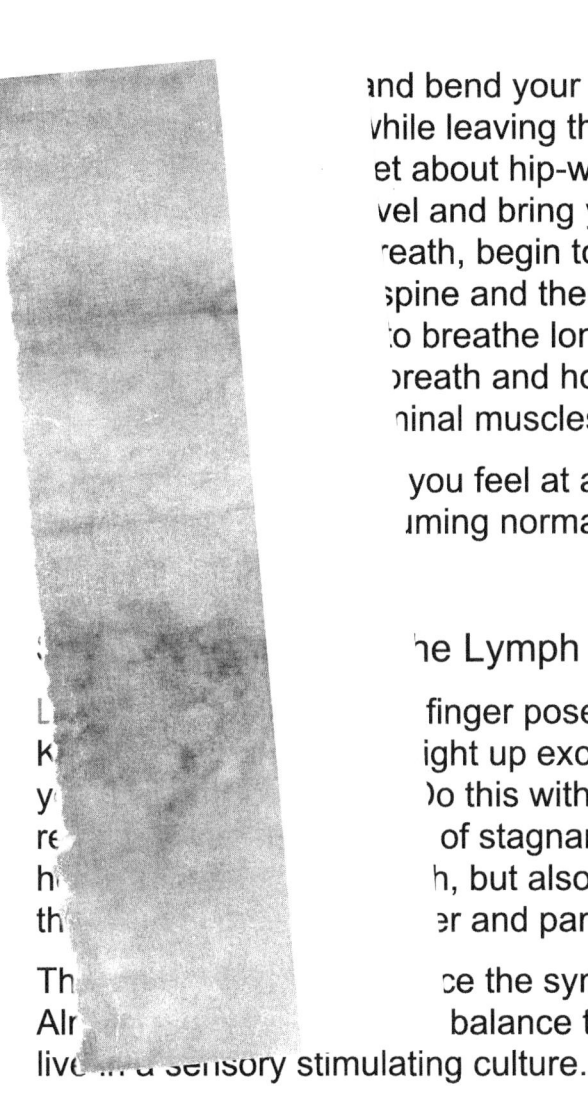

...nd bend your knees by raising them up to a
...vhile leaving the soles of your feet flat on the
...et about hip-width apart. Lay the palm of the
...vel and bring your attention to this part of the
...reath, begin to observe how the navel moves
...spine and then follow it upward as you inhale
...to breathe long and slow for 3-5 minutes and
...breath and how the navel is moving down and
...ninal muscles as you breathe.

...you feel at all light-headed, then wait a
...uming normal activities. Oxygenating the

...he Lymph

...finger pose to do for lymph congestion.
...ight up except the thumb that is touching
...Do this with both hands for 3-5 minutes
...of stagnant energies. This pose not only
...h, but also supports better metabolism in
...er and pancreas.

...ce the sympathetic nervous system.
...balance the nervous system because we
live ... a sensory stimulating culture.

Two other mudras that can be used to balance inner function;

Varuna Mudra is used to balance congestion in the sinuses, lungs or anywhere in the intestinal tract where irritation has stimulated the need for mucous. The GI tract is a key area where the lymph and the intestines work together to detox and maintain immune function. While this mudra is focused on balancing where there is irritation and mucous formation, it is named after Varuna, the god of water. This mudra helps to balance inner irritation and stress, thereby calming some of the inner linings and allowing for a smoother passage of fluids and substances within us.

Starting with the right hand, keep all fingers but the little finger and the thumb upright. Bend the little finger into the palm of the hand and place the ball of the right thumb on top of the little finger. Now wrap your left hand around your right so that the left thumb presses lightly into the right thumb little finger pose and the other fingers are gently wrapped around and supporting the right hand in the pose.

The author and well known mudra teacher, Gertrud Hirschi, indicates you can do this one for up to three times for forty-five minutes a day. Fewer repetitions for as little as 5-10 minutes of holding a position have brought noticeable relief to blocked passages.

Bhudi Mudra is specifically used for fluid balance in the whole body. Since the lymph is the body's major fluid system, this is a good one to support its function. Another easy mudra hand position to hold, it simply involves placing the tip of the little finger to the thumb while relaxing and widening the other fingers. Do this mudra for 15 minutes a day, as many as three times for greatest benefit. You can rest your hands on your thighs or furniture to allow holding the position to be relaxed.

Large Head Mudra will help to shift energy from accumulating in the head from all our busy thinking so that it circulates better. It balances by redistributing energy throughout the body.

Bring your thumb, index and middle finger together. Fold the ring finger down into the palm of the hand and let the pinky stand upright. This is also good for when you've been doing a lot of mental work or have a headache. It is recommended to hold the position for up to 6 minutes at a time.

This mudra is one of the best remedies for people who think a lot and tend to have a lot of their body's energy concentrated in their head. When I've used it for a headache I've actually held it for considerably longer and it has had a very good effect when something is making my head hurt.

Self-Help Thoracic Drainage

This is a simple, enjoyable way to improve flow in the major lymph drainage area of the body while relaxing, so what could be better? While lying down, place something really light across the collarbones (aka, the clavicles located right below the neck near the top of the shoulders). It could be your eyeglass holder, a small eye cover for sleeping (a filled one that is light) or a sock that has been stuffed with a plastic bag with about a half cup of grain or salt). This protocol lays something over the collarbones as a relaxing way to apply light pressure to open these lymph ducts that are the major drains in the body. It helps to improve the lymph flow overall, by opening up these major drains back into the venous circulation. As an added side benefit, it also helps to relieve sinus issues.

This protocol is from John Ossipinski. I like to do it as though I am the practitioner, with my left hand comfortably behind the back of my head and my right hand (with fingers wide spread) resting lightly across my clavicle bones. It feels reassuring and it works for me. Another way that I really enjoy doing this is to use both hands, spread out in fan fashion, left over right over the clavicle bones while lying down. With hands lightly resting on my body, it is a wonderfully comforting way to open the thoracic area and allow tight areas to open and increase their function, while enjoying greater relaxation. This is such an important center to open, since the heart is in this area, that it really should be the first one that you do. Once you do this, congestion in this area will be lessened, and this major lymph duct will be more ready to drain all that is flowing into it.

The first time I did this one, it was as if a layer of old armor lifted off, I felt so at ease. If this protocol is done with a slow, full breathing pattern, then both the relaxing and fluid circulation effects are increased. It's a win, win, win!

Self-Help Lymph in the Upper Body

Acupuncturist Suzanne Sky shared an exercise that she learned from her naturopath to stimulate lymph in the chest and underarm area. Since most modern women wear constricting garments around the chest, this is a great way to do something to open the chest up and stimulate better lymph function in an area that is slightly bound much of the day.

Stand upright and keep your feet no more than hip-width apart. Bring both arms out so that they are parallel to the floor. With palms down, begin to move the arms so that they are making small circles. Do ten circles in one direction and ten in the opposite direction. Then begin a new round by making slightly larger circles. Do both directions ten times each. Finally, widen the circle again until it's large and do ten repetitions. Reverse in the other direction to complete. It can be repeated two or three times in a day to boost the lymph function.

Another easy practice for women especially is to press the hands together in front of the chest (without a bra) for 5-10 presses to stimulate movement in the breast area. A daily practice of getting this tissue to move with this easy contracting exercise will help keep stagnation from setting in. Most women in the West are wearing a bra most of the time they are active; when it's off, most of us are not moving much to stimulate circulation.

Self-Help at the Digestive Center

The cisterna chyli is a place where three major rivers, or vessels, of the lymph system converge in the abdominal area below the sternum. An easy mudra hand position that will help to bring better energy flow to this area is known as the Mukula mudra or beak hand position.

Mukula Mudra position is made by bringing the tips of the fingers together so they resemble a beak. This concentrates the natural flow of healing energy into an area that is deficient or congested. Simply place your 'beak' fingers on the body to transfer energy and encourage better balance. To support the lymph vessels, nodes and capillaries in the abdominal area, first do the beak position with both hands right below the sternum for 3-5 minutes. Remember that any position you do, try to hold your hands in as relaxed a manner as possible. After holding this area for a few minutes, move down to the navel area and do another 3-5 minute round. If you have any area in the abdomen that feels a bit sluggish or uncomfortable, the beak will help to restore balance if you hold it over the area resting lightly. If there's something longstanding, then you'll likely have to make it a regular practice of adding in healing input to achieve more body ease. This is a very simple and effective way to get stagnant energy moving in the body.

The digestive part of our body is greatly challenged with the kinds of substances that we are exposed to through foods, products we use and the environment. Autoimmune disorders are sharply on the rise, and one of the strong possibilities for this trend has to do with adulterated substances and manmade toxins in just about everything we come into contact with.

As an example, my sweetie and I went to a nearby park one summer afternoon to enjoy the outdoors. We plunked ourselves down on a hillside of grass, and I began to notice that the blades in this area looked quite dehydrated. I did a quick scan to see if there were any signs of pesticide spraying, but there was no flag marker evident. After a few minutes I began to put together the clues and realized that the park's landscapers had sprayed the area to kill off the grass and neglected to put up any warnings. This part of the hillside is located just a few feet from a popular children's play area. I did confirm later that the landscapers had used a pesticide. With a smile the supervisor mentioned how they had used Roundup to kill off the plants in the whole hillside in short order. I thought to myself how he was happy that it was saving them work, but at what potential cost to health, to them and anyone else that takes in this neurotoxin?

Even low levels of chemical poisons require the body to use precious resources to rid itself of them, involving work of the lymph, liver, kidneys and the immune system. The more the immune system is turned on to defend itself, the greater the likelihood that it will lose its ability to differentiate correctly and begin making mistakes, as metabolic and environmental waste builds up internally.

I've known for a long time that it's not at all good to be exposed to this systemic poison, but information is now surfacing about how it may degrade intestinal function. Whatever the research that continues to specifically emerge on Roundup, our bodies are indeed too bombarded by chemicals. While exposure to one or two chemical toxins may not do significant damage, the overall level of exposure is increasing. Studies that have sampled the umbilical cord blood of newborns have shown that many babies have more than 200 industrial chemicals and pollutants at birth. Stored environmental toxins can be a significant handicap to proper development, let alone reaching one's full potential.

Giving the digestive area more attention with the beak mudra will help all of the digestive capillaries, vessels, nerves, organs, tissues and fluids to relax and be more flowing in accomplishing its work on our behalf. We all have universal energy flowing through us, so mudras are a simple way to provide positive input to the body. Allowing time daily to do an energy soothing and nourishing protocol may well bring more ease after a few days or a week.

Because the digestive center of the body often holds a lot of bound-up emotional energy, doing this mudra may bring about some emotional releases as well. Emotional energy movement is good for health, so it is suggested to acknowledge the feelings in motion as a good thing. We want to improve the flow of energy throughout the body to increase well-being.

Self-Help Lymph Reflexes on the Feet

This easy practice can help to restore more openness in the lymphatic reflexes located on the feet allowing more movement of fluids. Lymph reflexes begin where the toes meet the top of the foot, and they run between the tendons, so there are four reflexes on each foot in lines going up the foot toward the leg.

With the lymph, a soft touch is right. Stroke softly using four fingers in lines running straight up from the points between the toes. From the upper part of the foot, then continue with the fingers around the ankle and on up into the lower shin and calf. Move slowly with a flowing motion and repeat about 3-4 times on each foot.

Self-Help Windshield Wipers (aka, ScissorKicks)

This exercise is one of the simplest and the best for moving energy and fluids. While it was originally designed to boost the pumping action of the cerebrospinal fluid, this exercise is one that helps body fluids to circulate better, including the all-important lymph. Energy can pool at the feet and may need a bit of help sometimes to come back up, so this practice can energize someone who is tired. It's also another activity that reminds me of the simplicity of childhood and takes me away from my adult mindset.

Windshield Wipers Lying down, place your legs body-width apart. Begin moving your feet so that they move back and forth like windshield wipers on a car. Like laughing, this one usually stimulates a feeling of being a child again, carefree and having fun. This practice is good because you can do it while watching television or talking and have a positive stimulus while multitasking, in a good way!

Alternately, you can lie down on your stomach and rest your head into your folded arms. With your thighs on the floor, bend your knees and lift your legs up and allow them to do the wipers by crossing one leg over the other, then reversing the other way in a flowing fashion for 5 or more minutes. The stomach version of the posture also helps open the sinuses and the pelvis. If you have any back issues though, the first method is easier on the back.

Self-Help Dailies

Acupressure discs

When you need a bit of a boost from too much sitting in meetings, riding in a car or being glued to a computer screen, acupressure discs can improve the flow of energy through the body's meridians. While the first priority is to actually move the body and breathe deeply, these state-of-the-art holographic discs, about the size of a nickel, from Winning Factor, can be used to augment energy movement through the body's meridians. The Peak Performance discs were designed primarily for athletes to do their best when under pressure to perform, but they also work well in daily life. These discs increase circulation through the body's meridians and enhance energy movement within the physical body, such as the blood and lymph systems. Easy to use, a disc can be carried in a pocket to help keep an even flow of energy throughout the day.

Stand tall

All the practices that get you moving and that work to balance mind and body also support the body's ability to be upright with more ease and grace. I recall right after doing some qigong how much easier it was to maintain better carriage. I felt more internal strength that showed in being naturally more upright. I was also aware I felt more at home and centered in my own body, a most enjoyable experience.

Good posture is an overlooked but important way that we can help our lymph system to do its work. When the skeleton is aligned and moving with ease, it supports better circulation within. Like a twisted hose, the water doesn't flow as well when the hose is continually bent. The same is true for places in the body, such as the lymph capillaries and vessels, that have become hindered from poor posture. So remember that alignment is important for the body to fulfill its function to keep its fluids flowing and doing a good job of maintaining health.

Chair poses

For daily life, here are a couple of good stretches to break up the effects of being too sedentary. If you're sitting and working, these stretches will help to boost circulation.

1. Sitting up straight in a chair, with feet flat on the ground, raise your arms to be even height with your shoulders and bring your palms straight up and hold for some seconds.

2. Follow this with leaning back, allowing your back to be supported by the back of the chair, and let your hands hang behind the chair while opening the chest and arching your head back as far as comfortable. If it feels right, you can joint your hands together behind you to complete the stretch.

These two poses can be alternated to break up the tissue crystallization that tends to occur from sitting, most likely a bit stoop-shouldered, in front of a desk or computer screen. This helps to open up the upper body. Since the thoracic outlet, where the lymph fluid from most of the body empties back into the venous system, is in the collarbone area, this form of stretching helps to open this area up, freeing tissue and internal fluid movement. We may not notice that we're stiffening up as we age, but being sedentary does hinder the flow. There's a rhythm to body movement as muscle expansion and contraction occurs that encourages flow in neighboring lymph vessels, nodes and ducts.

3. The final pose is to do side turns. Start by crossing your legs. Turn your body toward the side of the top leg. For example, if your top leg is the right, then turn to the right side of the chair to stretch. With the right arm, hold the side of the chair to help steady the pose, while the left arm rests on the top leg. Hold for a several seconds, then reverse the pose. Do this a few times to open up the upper body and release tension from sitting. Cross stretches help to open the body up and counter tension being held.

Self-Help Massage and Aromatherapy

Massage is a practice aimed at increasing circulation and energy flow, with greater well-being as a result. Combining self-massage with essential oils, the good effect is multiplied. Touching with care is one of the most ancient forms of rejuvenation. From the time we come here as babies, caring touch helps us to develop in healthy ways, and as adults, it is no less important. Doing a little ritual like this and giving yourself time to relax and unwind by using the power of your own hands to softly stroke and caress your own skin is, in my opinion, one of the best forms of self-care.

Use a light touch that is continuous to remind the body of fluid movement. The intention is to be mindful and caring for the body in a nurturing way. Because so much of the lymph system's vast network of capillaries are below the surface of the skin, it's an easy way to lightly stimulate more circulation. As you probably know, the skin is our largest organ of elimination, so a massage serves a dual purpose to bring your own healing touch to the skin and the lymph capillaries that are close to the surface.

Aromatherapy can be used both to boost detox and to help the body to relax, depending on your intention. Warm the oil mix slightly by placing it in a container over some hot or warm water for a few minutes. It will release some aroma to begin the session. As a sensual experience, a warm oil massage can be a delightful antidote to stress.

For detox directly on the body, add 2-5 drops of one or more essential oils to one cup of carrier oil, such as almond, sesame, apricot or avocado before applying. If you haven't used an essential oil or blend before, it's best to start small, with 1-2 drops. If you are sensitive, you might even try it out on a small patch of the skin to check the effect that a particular oil or blend has, before going for the higher infusion or a body-wide application. Aromatherapy is a wonderful way to shift our psyche and body processes, so don't underestimate its potency.

Another option is to place drops directly into a diffuser and allow the oil to be taken in through breathing the oil-infused air. Because your aim is to nurture and detox, make sure the oils are of a high quality. Choose the company carefully to give yourself the best benefit. If you haven't used oils much, they are powerful, and it's best to be gentle in practice. When detoxing, I've found that people tend to want to stay with it when they don't have big healing events. Our bodies already are overloaded; a big detox at once can be another stressor. The goal is to feel better, and taking ongoing steps is a good way to go so that cleansing *feels* like it's a good thing, not a burden.

Some of the best oils for detox include bay laurel, rosemary, juniper, grapefruit, lemon, black cumin, myrtle and rose geranium. The laurus nobilis plant is well known for the use of its leaves in cooking. The bay laurel essential oil is also a highly effective lymph and immune system stimulant. Master aromatherapist Dr. Kurt Schnaubelt recommends using a few drops of the bay laurel essential oil directly on swollen lymph nodes to promote circulation and help these filters to open and drain. Experiment gingerly, as it were. Again, consider a small test before going full-on with any oil.

Another stimulating essential oil that promotes proper lymph function is the ever-popular rosemary. Beloved by bees and chefs worldwide, this universal herb also stimulates good blood flow in the brain and brings a refreshing effect on one's perspective. A lesser known oil, cypress, also promotes proper lymph function by supporting cell health and the ability of the body to clear cellular debris effectively from the body.

Acting as a diuretic, both juniper and grapefruit improve the body's ability to eliminate toxins, taking some of the burden off the lymph system. Lemon is helpful for the liver, one of the body's primary organs of detoxification. The liver has more than 500 functions in the body, so lightening its load brings a big benefit to improve function. Lemon also helps the lymph to function better.

Rose geranium oil works primarily with the liver and kidneys, both organs that work to clean the blood and fluids of toxins. Because the liver and lymph work so closely to handle inner toxins and foreign substance removal, when one area receives a boost to efficiently handle waste, it helps the other. The citrus smell of mandarin oil helps people to relax while bolstering the vital function of the liver to work in tandem with the lymph. Both helichrysum and lemongrass help to improve lymph drainage.

Lightly massage the oil blend into as much of your body as possible and make it a relaxing way to be in touch, bringing appreciation to the body for all it does. Another way to improve lymph health is to do dry body brushing before beginning the oil massage to stimulate lymph movement (See Self-Help Dry Skin Brushing below for a fuller description). Body brushing also gives a very positive stimulus for body circulation since so much of the peripheral lymph system is close to the surface of the skin. Remember to brush always toward the chest and upper thoracic area, since this major lymph return is under the collarbones.

Once you've done this healthy ritual, either finish with a warm shower or bath to soak, or wrap yourself up in something warm and rest for a while in a peaceful spot to give yourself a mini spa treatment and let the touch and oils complete their inner work of improving circulation and helping the body to offload waste through proper lymph drainage. Improving circulation also helps the lymphocytes to move more easily throughout the body to do their work of protecting us.

Anytime you're initiating a detox, it's good to drink a good amount of pure water, and hydrating and green foods to help the body complete its work of clearing toxins and metabolic debris. Movement will also support the body's ability to eliminate what is no longer wanted or needed internally while detoxing.

Self-Help Dry Skin Brushing

Since so much of the peripheral lymph system is under the skin, dry skin brushing is one of the best methods of improving circulation and drainage of the lymph. It is also one of the most readily available practices. Like all practices, finding the right groove to do it and become consistent is key. Ron Teegarden, the master Asian herbalist, was once asked what is the best practice. He replied, "One that you will do." I heartily agree.

While working to improve the flow in life, it's a good to experiment with different ways of assisting the body, until we find ones that we know are best for us. Dry brushing is effective and it's easy to do in a few minutes, which makes it more likely that it can fit into one's daily schedule.

Brushing does not take a lot to learn. The key aspects are these:

- Use a natural bristle brush that is firm, and apply it with light strokes to the body before showering. The goal is a light exfoliation and stimulation, not to make the skin red or irritated.
- Start at the feet and make your way up the body with long smooth strokes.
- Move up from the bottom of the trunk to the upper chest moving toward the upper thoracic area. A longer brush will make it easier to do strokes on the back. Complete the brushing on the body at the collarbones in the center. This is where the major lymph ducts drain back into the circulatory system.
- From the shoulders, stroke down the body to the collarbones. If you stroke the neck, be very gentle and remember to move the brush downward, since this is the path of drainage. Few experts discuss brushing the face, but if you do, use a soft bristle brush and stroke gently.
- Beginning at the fingers, move up the arm to where it joins the shoulder/chest area. If you'd like you can stroke to the collarbone area.

Nadine Artemis of Living Libations suggests putting a drop of some kind of botanical oil onto the natural bristle brush and then gently brushing all over. Since much of the body's vast system of lymph capillaries are found right under the top layer of skin, the light stimulation of dry brushing provides impetus to unclog areas that have not had enough hydration or movement to keep the lymph system open and flowing.

While finishing this book, I came across a new book on dry brushing. The author, Mia Campbell, has proposed different ways to do this technique. One of her suggestions, rather than start at the feet and work your way up to the heart, it may be better to start at the collarbones and activate this area first because the two largest portals for the lymph fluids to return to the blood circulatory system are located under these bones. It makes a lot of sense that if you're going to increase flow that will eventually reach this major return portal, then first open up the largest area of drainage so it can accommodate the increased volume to come. She based this recommendation on the work that lymph specialists do when working to open up lymph movement. Having experimented with this, I think she's on to something.

At present I am starting at the area of the return junction, the collarbones, lightly brushing each collarbone from each end to the center to activate it. I start on the left side with the main return junction. The brush bristles are firm and my intention is to make contact to awaken, but not the pressure of a scrubbing action. Then I do several of the areas where the largest clusters of nodes are near the surface of the skin. First, I brush down the neck lightly, since a large number of the body's node defense filters are here.

Then I raise my arm and lightly brush the crease inside of the elbows, then move to the armpit area to stimulate this cluster of nodes (both sides, left first). Next, I go down to each foot and stroke upward where the lymph reflexes are on the top of the foot between the toes. I lightly stroke at the top of the foot where the ankle is. Then I go to the back of the knee where nodes are clustered and brush upward. I brush upward at the inguinal areas that are located in the crease where the leg joins the body. First, do the area just below the crease, then above it on the body. Then take the brush from the outer pubic area and draw it toward the centerline of the body and brush up to the collarbones. I do the right side, then the left side where the major return is.

Finally, I lightly brush the collarbones again, first right then ending with the left. This routine feels right for now. Starting first and brushing the collarbones to activate this major lymph return feels like a great breakthrough. Her book, listed in the Resources section, has a well-developed dry brushing protocol if you decide to work more with this practice.

Having worked with a light pinching technique modeled after the hands on work that my cranial osteopath did on my neck, I can say that many months later, the nodes in this area are vastly less 'nodular.' I attribute it not only to the hands-on work, but to use of cranberry and enzymes to assist the lymph system in its work as well. While I've read that it was once taboo to touch the nodes and probably still is today in some circles, I felt empowered after her firm and rhythmical way of lightly tugging on the nodes while moving down my neck. She told me the nodes were sluggish, so I decided then to help them do their work more readily. Now I mostly just brush lightly down the neck to stimulate this area lightly as part of the dry brushing practice.

A few minutes spent dry brushing is a very easy and positive stimulus to the skin, the body's largest organ of elimination. Dry skin brushing clears the skin of dead cells and helps to unclog pores on the surface to promote healthy glowing skin. It also stimulates oil-secreting glands embedded in the skin's layers, thereby helping to moisturize the skin.

With just a few minutes a day, it can work wonders to activate the lymph system to get moving so it can properly drain waste from the body. A big proponent of dry brushing, Dr. Lemole has indicated that it is also a way to help the nervous system to renew itself. This one practice is a way to get a lot of benefit in 5-10 minutes. I say get that brush and get going!

As with all things, use common sense; if you have an area with broken skin, varicose veins, rash, edema, or any infection, avoid using the brush on these surfaces. If you have any kind of degenerative condition or a health issue consult a qualified medical or health practitioner about the feasibility of your doing dry skin brushing.

Self-Help Sweating

Sweating is a very effective way to move toxins out through the pores of the skin quickly and help the lymph system by offloading a good measure of toxic material that would otherwise need to be transported. Because too many sedentary ways contribute to a build-up of internal toxicity, sweating is a way to kick-start a sizable purging of inner pollutants.

While a sauna is effective, it's not for everyone, nor is it to be taken lightly. I've had to learn this the hard way. Visiting a Korean spa salt room, I was so enjoying what I thought was the right amount of heat that I stayed in one of the chambers for over an hour. It triggered a cleanse that lasted for weeks.

For anyone with heart or blood pressure issues or any medical condition, it would be best to let your doctor determine if even a short sauna or a steam is a good way to detox. Because heat will increase your heart rate, make sure you're ready for this very effective form of cleansing.

Another fairly accessible way to get a good jump on detoxing is a steam bath. With many gyms and spas offering rooms for steam infusion, this is a way to wash out a lot of toxins in a short period of time. The heat opens up pores in the skin, dilates blood and lymph vessels, gets the heart going, and gives the body a good opportunity to offload a good measure of waste in a relatively short period of time.

Having worked with cleanses for quite a while, slow and gentle works. Finding practices that you can do consistently are really effective ways to improve health.

Self-Help Water Cures

Water is a universal healer, so it is a resonant way to promote better function in the fluid based system of lymph. Water cures help the body to relax and clear constriction in its vessel and muscular tissue systems that have a direct impact on lymph function. Spa therapies are also helpful for the nervous system to relax and engage more of the parasympathetic function with a good effect system wide. Finally, since the lymph works with detox, the use of water therapies can literally make us of the skin as the body's largest organ of elimination to take a load off the lymph.

One way to have a bit of spa therapy at home to nurture and detox is to make a hot bath with Epsom salts. Add three cups of the Epsom salts to the bath. Magnesium sulfate is a great way to take in more magnesium and help the body to relax more. Many doctors have indicated that Americans are not getting enough of this anti stressor mineral. Fill the tub so you can soak for about twenty minutes for the best effect.

Julia Loggins, author of *Dare to Detoxify*, offers another version of a bath spa treatment: Add a half pound of sea salt and a quarter cup of baking soda to a hot bath, and soak for half an hour. Sea salt is a very effective way to help the body flush toxins and restore natural balance. Baking soda is a natural alkalizer that is helpful, according to Loggins, in countering the effect of radiation in the body. Again, give yourself a time to wind down after detoxing in your spa tub retreat. The body needs to have time to rejuvenate and recover from so many stressors.

Another way to bring more stress relief is to add 5-10 drops of an essential oil to the bath. Lavender is a tried-and-true calming agent, as are chamomile and sandalwood, to add other botanical notes of relaxation to the heat and enveloping water. There are a lot of essential oil-infused salt combinations now with oils already added that promote detox. Just look for pure and simple ingredients that you recognize.

Again, if there are any heart, blood pressure or contraindicated medical conditions, don't begin a protocol like this without medical advice, just to be safe. Afterward, lightly dry off and wrap yourself up in something warm and cozy. Either time it so you can go straight to sleep at night, or take some kind of uninterrupted rest for the body to receive the full spa reward of detoxing with relaxation and renewal. (Consider doing the Vajrapradama mudra with this for a great relaxing boost, located in The Heart as GPS.)

It's best to have both the bath and shower water filtered, given the amount of metals and chemicals that are still in many water systems. This way, you're not being exposed to more pollutants as you are giving yourself a spa treatment to rejuvenate.

As with the spa 'taking of waters,' our inner fluids are a rejuvenating system of cleansing and nourishing and revitalizing. As we learn to go with the flow of what works for lymph function, we can realize increased well-being in many ways. Any time we do anything to stimulate detox, it is always recommended to hydrate internally with pure water.

There are many effective European water treatments that combine detox and sensory enjoyment for a rejuvenating effect. A simple one that can be done at home is to alternate hot and cold showering. The heat opens pores and dilates vessels and increases circulation and the cold then causes a contraction. The rhythm of the alternating hot and cold gets more movement going internally, as well, to eliminate waste. This form of water treatment is also helpful for the nervous system. This protocol helps to reset it and turn down sympathetic activation, allowing the calming and restorative parasympathetic system to guide the body's function.

[4]
Living Life in the Flow

Free circulation of blood, lymph, energy, thoughts and feelings is important to the vitality and health of our body, mind, heart and spirit and to the immune system.

Elson Haas

The inner fluid volume inside the body is a precious resource. As it circulates through us, it takes on various forms and labels. Four of the major ones include: blood plasma, interstitial fluid, cerebrospinal fluid and lymph fluid. While each form of fluid has a different composition of elements, it is all one fluid system moving within, mostly made of water. We call it fluid as a substance, but this is also a description of its ability to move and flow and change and adapt. The purpose of this book is to highlight the inner terrain known as the lymph system, which is mostly fluid, and help us to develop more awareness of it, as well as the right relationship with our 'longevity juice' system.

Living our lives, as Dr. Haas has so aptly stated, we need to take all of our fluidic elements into consideration, including the 'water' element of emotions and feelings and the 'air' element of our thoughts. We have seen that the motion of breathing, an aspect of the air element, is a key impetus for the fluid system to move and circulate. As a whole system, we need to consider how we are intact on all levels—mind, body, heart and spirit—learning to find more balance and harmony.

The composition of our internal and unseen 'rivers' of fluid has a direct impact on the quality of life, even if we don't know much about this mysterious matrix, composed mostly of water. A polluted pond within is not a foundational resource to allow our bodies, let alone our lives, to thrive and flourish. The body is meant to have a considerable volume of water that is capable of cleansing internally. Think of how clean you would feel if you were trying to take a shower with one plastic bottle of water. It wouldn't go very far. Not having enough fluid to do its job is a major—even if unrecognized—stress to the body. As Dr. Cousens pointed out decades ago, there is a chemistry to stress, and it isn't a chemical broth that promotes longevity. In order to survive and thrive, we need to make some different choices and learn the value of course-correcting our lives over time.

I've had a number of wake-up calls throughout my life, and I've learned to heed the warnings more readily. The appendix wake-up call mentioned in the beginning of this book was one of the largest of my life. I realized that I had to alter my emotional way of living even more than how I was treating my body. For me, this 'healing crisis' came from too many years of tamping down festering feelings that led to my body not being able to cope with the physical detox process I had been doing for a couple of months. Even with how arduous it was, I had a profound admiration for my own system and the intelligence that was doing its best to offload a toxic burden that had built up, much of it having to do with the acidic chemistry that was a result of stress from suppressing a lot of feelings for a long, long time.

When I've done physical cleansing, it has always brought with it a good cleanse emotionally. This time, I was aware that there was a lot of crystallized emotion, but there was much more that had been buried. My body's response was to try to clean house and clear out a lot of residue in this one event.

Over and over in my life, if I begin to have physical symptoms, there is very often some mental or emotional aspect that needs attending to help my body unwind from the stress of feelings or thoughts that have not been resolved. When my mind is running rampant, I usually don't feel so good in my form. I feel ill at ease. Once I am able to contact the core of the situation, then the physical symptoms seem to subside rather quickly. I've learned to drop in the question to ask my body what burden it would like to let go of and to be as patient as possible while the response becomes clear to me on a conscious level. With this, I've had the wonderful benefit of experiencing a sense of peace more often, as inner conflicts and disturbances that are identified as emotional or mental are resolved and surrendered.

I'm sharing this to show a little of how I've worked with the impact that my thoughts and feelings have on my body. We're really a whole system with some different 'parts,' but our inner governing system doesn't separate or compartmentalize the way we do in our heads. Many doctors now recognize that the mind-body connection is quite real and valid, from the pioneering work of Dr. Bernie Segal to two doctors featured in this guide, Dr. Lemole and Dr. Haas. Dr. Haas' book, *Staying Healthy with the Seasons*, was my first introduction to a convergence of Eastern and Western forms medicine, and this has had a lasting influence on believing in the best of both worlds.

This book is meant to encourage some experimenting to expand perspective, as any creative person does. We are all creative sparks, and we should allow ourselves to be 'inspirited' with awareness and to make use of it in our lives. To do this allows us to feel more alive, vibrant and fulfilled. We are meant to try things out and find out what works and what doesn't, and to move forward with greater awareness of our authenticity. Theologian Matthew Fox identifies the experience of becoming more authentic as a form of grace, to realize more of our true nature.

We first grew in the amniotic environment of our mother's womb. As adults, we've come to find out, we are still immersed in water. One of the primary waterways within is the lymph system. It works constantly to carry elements to nourish the cells, bring messages to regulate life, haul away many kinds of waste, and do its best to maintain fluidic equilibrium. It helps in some way to visualize this inner body of water as a kind of aquarium that both feeds and takes the waste into its watery solution. The aquarium, although it is basically invisible to us, needs certain additions to allow what is alive within it to thrive. Because most of the inner working is quite invisible, we can easily forget that to function well or at all, we still need to provide our inner aquarium with healthy resources to have a reasonable possibility of living a long and full life.

So this guide is meant to help us clarify and strengthen our intentions about living well and to experiment and discover what works for us in a deeper way that we can commit to with more dedication. When we find what resonates best with our heart, the inner compass, then it will guide us better than all the advice from experts alone. So this last section is focused on the water element, with its qualities of love and care and compassion, and on finding more peace with how we live through uniting head and heart, and balancing the air and water elements within.

Stress is a part of life because we all face challenges and pressure. Making healthy choices provides positive momentum to lessen stress that can become distress. Unresolved stress takes a huge toll on our capacity to function and maintain living systems. Fluids and tissues are constricted by unresolved stress, so when we free our hearts and minds, we are creating a huge impetus to allow the rightful flow and function of the well-designed lymph to care for us.

Feeling Fully Alive

Many of us would like to feel vitally alive, but it seems somehow beyond our reach. Publications tout it, but how do we embody feeling alive? For me, these peak states are always characterized by a sense of flow and connection, within and without, that feels quite true to who I am. I could say that feeling fully alive is a coming home kind of experience, of having embraced more of who I am and having met with compassion part of what I was but no longer need to be. I've let go of something that was frozen in place but is now free to be surrendered. In its stead, I definitely feel more vital. The experience of being more vital is expressed on the micro level, as our bodies are able to surrender the old waste and allow in nutrients, of oxygen and food substances, within a watery milieu that is life-supporting.

In daily practice, I find that making sounds with movement is a great way to release held tension and bring more vital oxygen into the body. Listening to music and intuitively moving and making sound with it is a highly underrated form of stress-relieving therapy that is fun and effective. One of my tried and true favorites is the childhood favorite of 'blowing raspberries.' When life is frustrating and I've spent too long at the computer screen without solving a problem, I get up and wave my arms around and blow some raspberries to clear the energy and get a fresh start.

I learned the arm-moving portion of this from an ophthalmologist visit decades ago. He mentioned that I had severe eye nerve strain caused by a lot of up-close computer work. He suggested that I get up once an hour and move around and wave my arms to assist my nervous system in integrating all the information I was trying to 'digest.' It helped.

Just remember, our animal bodies need to move, to make sounds and let go of whatever has been constricting it. Picture how you've seen dogs shake things off. Most of us have learned to 'quiet down' since childhood in one way or another. Singing in the shower and the car and letting out some enthusiastic energy is a great way to reconnect with a flow and help to unblock areas of tension. With this, we can help our tissues to be freer to move internal fluids and make it easier to get on with keeping the body humming along. One of my favorite lines is from the poet Walt Whitman; "I sing the body electric." Expression through sound and movement are more than luscious sounding words, they actually work to charge up our spiritual batteries so that our bodies are more enlivened.

Laughter and Joy

Laughing can have a positive effect on immune function, the lymph system's close partner, but does it directly help the lymph system? Well, recall that stress has a detrimental effect on the lymph function, constricting the vessels. Also, with stress, we tend to breathe more shallowly. The body registers this lack of oxygen as additional stress, so this can create a vicious circle, from the body not having what it needs: oxygen and more ease. If breathing is restricted, so is stimulation of the lymph. Laughter, as a belly laughing experience, opens us up and brings expansion to meet the contraction of stress and held tension. Obviously, it is a great way to breathe more deeply with a lot more enjoyment.

A special form of yoga has evolved called laughter yoga or Hasyayoga. This form of yoga was developed in 1995 and has proven to be a great way to increase oxygenation as well as more body ease. Like the lymph, laughter is highly underrated and it can easily be overlooked in our multi-tasking world. With the intensity and responsibilities of life we need to counterbalance the buildup of tension and crystalized ways of being with enjoyable 'remedies' such as laughing.

A recommendation to laugh more to support the lymph actually comes from one of the country's foremost lymph experts, Dr. Chikly. It spontaneously increases breathing, a boon for lymph circulation. Even better, according to Dr. Chikly, it is a most enjoyable way to open up the largest lymph return channel in the front of the body, the thoracic duct. His prescription: laugh long and deep and get your lymph going!

Finding things that are sweet and inclusive to laugh about reinforces connectedness and relieves stress in many ways. Laughing may be the most enjoyable way to help out our highly challenged lymph system to become more fluid, with increased body ease. It's a win-win practice for sure. Author and vibrant food and lifestyle expert David Wolfe says it well: "The world is made young with laughter." So are we.

This next practice comes from yoga and meditation teacher Soraya Saraswati, and it's too good to pass up—jump for joy! She suggests, and I concur, that jumping and letting out our inner child to play and dance and whoop it up is a great way to stay in tune with ourselves as physical beings that are vessels for happiness and joy. In the day-to-day humdrum and the ten thousand things, most of us have lost our connection with an inner sense of delight and discovery. One way we might 'elevate' ourselves is through play with jumping rope, a way to connect again with childlike happiness. I used to love jumping around puddles or running around when a warm spring or summer rain came down. It was quite enlivening.

I'll never forget seeing a young boy leaping in the air and whooping it up during a heavy rainstorm in Ohio. Witnessing his celebratory being in the moment is an indelibly-etched impression. Having children to actually play with is one of the best ways to tap into the world of present-centered happiness with movement forms of play. We need to practice going against the grain of being too task-oriented and trying to be on target all the time. Indulging in a bit of play can help us to remember the spice in life. It may not only activate our lymph, but also bring a big spontaneous smile of happiness, a great side benefit in the often-weary world of adult concerns.

Get Happy

The field of positive psychology is a rapidly expanding, much needed antidote to the toll that life can take. Making use of its insights is a very timely way to harness more proactive momentum within the whole system that we are, through learning to generate more harmony in our inner workings. It's time to have more ways to catalyze better outcomes for our lives, so again, exploring to find what resonates is the right activity to engage in. Happiness corresponds with a sense of greater order and coherence, of inner circuitry working with ease. It is truly a flow state that is free.

One happiness expert is Tracey Cleantis, with her book, *The Next Happy: Let Go of the Life You Planned and Find a New Way Forward.* While she has ample clinical expertise, she is also openly honest in acknowledging that she's learned about what she calls the 'next happy' from her own experience as well. Tracey is a person who has embraced creative being. Creative people know that what we might call a 'mistake' can be an opening disguised as a challenge. If we are only focused on problems and keeping our life confined, then we may not be able to see a glimmer of the new peeking in through an outcome that is different from what we thought we wanted.

From a creative perspective, mistakes and challenges can be an opening into discovery of a whole new field of understanding of how we relate to life, how we work or the kinds of relationships we engage in. In daily life, however, we're so focused on getting everything right and never making a 'mistake' that we effectively block a lot of growth opportunities that can lead to forms of greater fulfillment of all types. Not to mention that we're effectively stopping a kind of flow in our lives, as the old saying goes, 'of one thing leading to another.'

One of the best writers on this subject is the spiritual minister, Temple Hayes. I was fortunate to interview her recently and she shared these words,

> What I've found is that everything we have endured in our lives, everything we walk through, we are meant to become more of ourselves on the other side. I have more energy in my fifties than I did in my thirties because I live by the belief that whatever happens--even something as profound as my father dying unexpectedly in a tragic way--even in the midst of that grief, I decided to make my father's life matter. I'm going to make the experience matter and out of that I'm going to become more, not less. I really believe that, and I live life that way.

I really agree with Temple and her approach has been used many times to take something that is rather unwieldy and use it as an ingredient to make something *much* better as an outcome.

I live by doing my best to see outside the box of daily habitual thinking to a more abundant and creative perspective. It's a very fine form of 'adaptive re-use,' to envision how something can find another life in a new setting as I shift my perspective. Learning to handle what comes and make something positive from it is a good way to increase the quotient of happiness.

Make it a priority to do something, however small, to bring some more delight into your life. One of my surefire ways to reset my day is to put on the YouTube video of Pharrell Willams's song "Happy." Waving my arms and hands to the beat and twirling around for a few minutes of simple joy is an effective restart when my energies begin to ebb such as when I've gotten caught in thinking life is one big problem. So find some music that brings a smile and let it have its way with your outlook on the day. Oh, and it's great for the lymph too, so just let go and *enjoy*.

Another way to up my quotient of happy feelings is to literally stop and smell a rose, a freesia or the sublime wisteria—whatever is blooming and available—and appreciate its beauty and aroma. For me it's instantaneous rejuvenation. If I'm wired, I can take my shoes off and let my feet touch the earth or go and plunk my bottom down on grass; before long, I feel grounded and more at ease. Recently I was feeling radiant, and a smile was beaming right out of me as I was walking somewhere. A stranger responded to it by thanking me. The gentleman let me know that he appreciated the sharing inherent in the smile. I had no motive for smiling at him, and it was so much fun to see how it was an offering to someone else's day. We all need nurturing and space to breathe easy to keep the *joie de vivre* in our lives, so I invite you to an experiment—to move away from the electronic screen that has you mesmerized and go find some more happy. Who knows where it might lead?

Heart Waves

The HeartMath Institute has done extensive long-term research on how to train the heart and mind to work together. They have found that the electromagnetic field of the heart is actually larger than that of the brain, suggesting that it perhaps is the more important organ to guide our function. Hmmm.

They found that the electrical activity of the heart (heart waves) is actually 40-60 times stronger than that of the brain. The research of HeartMath found that sincere experiences of appreciation, joy and caring, (i.e., the heartfelt emotions) led to an increased sense of coherence and generated a sense of well-being within.

The heart, as a lead organ to nourish the body through the blood, can also effectively entrain the brain toward more coherent function. In so doing, it lessens the habituated pattern of stress to contract muscles, send the mind racing (corresponding with increased activation of a nervous system sympathetic system response) and taking only shallow breaths. This circular pattern leads to more stress and less function.

When head and heart are not going in the same direction, stress is an expression of this inner disharmony. Since stress lessens the functioning of the lymphatic system, and it's already overloaded, we need to cultivate ways to release stress and build more strength to face the pressures of daily life.

Obstacles and challenges call us to rise up and become more authentic, acting as a spur to grow. To meet our challenges, we need to resource our lives. Spending some time each day cultivating a smile in our hearts will bring great rewards. As shown from the HeartMath research, when we spend time with self care practices, such as softly massaging the body and acknowledging it with appreciation, we are not only activating positive lymph flow, we're bringing the power of the heart to restore well-being within.

A quote from Dr. Stone sums it up: "The heart center with all the radiating energy is like a fountain which supplies the body with the water of life, the fire of warmth and the breath of life to sustain and rebuild and nourish all parts." The ultimate anti stressor is to bring the heart's energy of loving care into life.

Finding Stress Relief in Head-Heart Balance

Here's a mind body practice that you can use to help your heart do its work effectively to guide the mind. When experiencing something that is triggering a stress response, stop for a few moments and inhale and exhale deeply a couple of times. Visualize a big STOP sign that tells whatever circular thoughts are running amok that it's time to desist. When exhaling, let the body sink, rather than holding it taut with vigilance from whatever is upsetting in the moment. Keep doing the basic in and out breath long and deep, and focus on the breath moving in your body, not the thoughts running amok in your head. We've become accustomed to being at home in our heads and we need to be at home in the heart and body more.

Once you can feel your body beginning to soften a bit, then put your hands on your heart area (possibly doing the Vajrapradama mudra described below) and begin to recall a place of pure love, care, kindness or a moment of appreciation. Keep breathing in and out as fully as possible, to be in the moment with a different resonance. Set your intention to allow higher possibilities to result in a better outcome and surrender it into the breath and just be with it as much as possible.

You may even have a sudden welling up from your belly with a deep exhale as the body lets go of a burden of stress that is running over and over and depleting inner resources while taking its toll. This little exercise can work wonders, and the more you do it, the more entrained your body will be to let go and return to the present feeling more resourced. The mind/body movement discovered decades ago that imagining positively like this is quite real to your system, so let it work its magic and help bring the flowing movement of air in the form of the breath, easily received as the abundant resource it is meant to be, to let your body have the right supply that it is intended to have.

Simple practices can help us to engage in a more open way of meeting what happens in life. Play to find ones that work for you. Here are a few ways to use your imaginative ability to reset your response to something that is causing an inner stir. Remember the expansive sense of having abundant oxygen and air to meet challenges by opening a window to let in a fresh breeze, or actually go out into the open air and take a walk to promote a sense of proper circulation. Engaging in something that brings a sense of good movement and flow is a good time to recall a sense of freedom to make good choices. We can also pause for a moment and imagine an open window inside our minds when facing a challenge to allow better options to be received, since the universe has lots of potential if we but create more expansiveness to allow and receive. As one of my teachers, John Beaulieu, once said, "It's not a question of whether you'll have challenges in life, it's a matter of what you'll do to respond to them." Learning to meet life in a resourced way and being open and curious about the unfolding without being fixated on a particular outcome is a very creative way to engage with universal energy. Easier said than done, but the result is well worth the applied effort.

Here's an lovely way to practice breathing as a way to induce more calm from the highly revered Buddhist advocate of peace, Thich Nhat Hanh:

> Breathing in, I calm body and mind.
>
> Breathing out I smile.
>
> Dwelling in the present moment.

Smiling is good to help engage our inner neurotransmitters of positive flowing emotions. Another mind-heart integrating tradition comes from what is known as loving kindness meditation. This version comes from the great meditation teacher and author, Jack Kornfield:

> May I be filled with lovingkindness.
>
> May I be well.
>
> May I be peaceful and at ease.
>
> May I be happy.

It's important for stress relief to find ways to turn off the inner broadcast of negative thoughts and repetitive feelings 24/7. It's not so easy at times, but the body needs to be nurtured and reassured, and the turbulent barrage of thoughts that constantly careens inside our heads (with corresponding turbulent emotions) really takes a toll on our body's well-being and ability to maintain healthy equilibrium. One of the definitions of stress that I am most resonant with is that it arises from not being authentic. When we are barraged internally with negative thoughts, this can cause a crisis because it is interfering with knowing that we are worthy and deserving of the good.

I began chanting sacred words many years ago after having some great success with meditation to improve the peace of my inner landscape and turn down the 'noise' inside my head. It was a good adjunct to meditation that I could do silently as I went about my day to rewrite some inner mental programs that were disturbing me and bringing a constant sense of inner static. One fall day as I was working in the yard and enjoying nature's beauty, a very obsessive thought started racing around inside my mind. The noisy thought intruder was buzzing around inside my head like a loud mosquito.

Annoyed for a while, spontaneously I just responded to this intrusive part of my awareness and said to it internally, "You can go now or you can go when I do the mantra, but you *will* go." I had confidence in my chanting practice because at this point, I had been having much more peace from thoughts clanging around in the daily foray of life. Immediately the obsessive circling thought vanished. I smiled. Mantras using sacred words can support the heart and direct the mind into more peaceful paths as well. This loving kindness round is one of my favorites to accomplish this.

The Heart as GPS

I like to do the loving kindness meditation with a mudra that restores my heart.

This mudra is named *Vajrapradama*. While it has a long foreign sounding name, it's basically a sacred heart connector. I'll call it the heart mudra for ease of reference. Used over time, it will foster trust in your heart area and promote more sense of connectedness. In the life of speed and stress we most often live, this is a welcome balm, to be softly touching our tender heart area and holding this part of our body and inviting more openness. This simple and powerful mudra is basically a form of self-blessing, a way to feel more solidly anchored in the heart and the body because it fosters the feeling of safety. It is very effective in countering stress because feeling more connected to one's own heart, as well as feeling connected spiritually, will foster a greater sense of ease and well-being in the body and in life.

Heart Mudra Loosely interlace the fingers of both hands over your chest with your palms facing down on the body. Hold this pose softly, so find a way to relax your arms so that you're not bringing more tension through your arms and hands to the heart/chest area. I usually do this pose lying down. This pose is also good for your lymph system, since the thoracic duct is also located in this area. While in the pose, lightly touch your thumbs to the collarbones; as this will help to boost the openness of the major lymph ducts that are the portals for fluids to return to the blood circulation system. This is such a sweet and powerful way to open.

When you do this mudra, it may also allow for some pent-up energies to flow, so if it does, just let the emotional bath occur and then allow yourself to feel renewed from surrendering some spent emotional energy. Author of the book aptly titled *Mudras*, Gertrud Hirschi offers this affirmation to go with the mudra. I'm including it here, because it feels perfect:

> I am a creation of the greatest omnipotence, whose strength
> and power lovingly support me at all times.

Because the front of the upper body is such a vital center for lymph return and for overall flow within the body, we should incorporate daily practices that bring resources to this center. With the findings of the HeartMath research and work by other researchers on emotional intelligence, it behooves us to support the proper functioning of our heart space 'GPS' so that we can have the right orientation and access to higher intelligence in our lives. While the lymph does not have its own heart pump, it still requires us to bring heart energy to support its function and counteract the effects of stress on our fluid lymphatic system that diminish its function.

While life brings challenges and we often face issues that are not easy to resolve, simply grinding around with them is not the approach to live with basic wellness, let alone ease and enjoyment. Adversity and pain can be part of life, and we need to develop our own ways of adapting to difficulties by adding in practices that strengthen and bring new perspective. We also must take time away to renew ourselves and enjoy life, even in the face of difficulties, some of them prolonged and arduous.

A documentary film titled *Happy,* by director Roko Belic, makes the point that a lot of what we are chasing in our material culture does not really make us happy. With images of people around the globe, it shows that some of the happiest people around the world are actually the poorest. Despite their circumstances, they are happy with their families and grateful for all that they *do* have.

We get wrapped up in chasing a lot of 'bigger is better' pictures of life here in America, very much focused on what we do not have. It's a real irony that one of the richest countries in the world has so many citizens completely focused on their lack. We need to slow down the race to get to the next thing and the next. The film makes the point quite well with its visuals that a shift of perspective can be a very good thing. Often if we can stop and reflect, we find that all these 'things' are not what our heart is calling for us to focus on anyway.

Life is always a 'work in progress' because we are all creative forms that are changing. In order to realize happiness, we need to honestly answer the question, "How well do you want to live your own heart's desires?" Creative, intelligent problem solving is going on inside the body and brain all the time. Our bodies change at the micro level constantly. We need to align with the ability to change more consciously to make it a part of life for more constructive and enjoyable outcomes. Discovery and exploration are true keys to living a real life. We should enjoy more time not knowing and finding new answers and opening new doors of perception to remain fresh in how we are engaging in living.

While we think of the body as a bunch of organs, glands and vessels, the body is actually a coherent living system that we've divided up for the purpose of our understanding. We need to realize that it has great undivided intelligence that works to create unity in its operation 24/7, with very little thought involved consciously to keep it all going, so we should appreciate the wonder of this gift daily. There's so much acting in our favor each moment that we don't have to think too much about—such as being able to move and imagine and love.

As shown in the HeartMath research, bringing our awareness to the 'appreciation' channel is really good for health and wellbeing. As part of our daily practice, we should make it a habit to focus on what is working well and acknowledge it. Quite literally, it helps us to function more optimally to take a little time and bring attention to where there is health and keep smiling as much as possible. It promotes production of the right neurotransmitters so we have good functional flow of body systems within.

Dr. Sears has coined a phrase about 'making health your hobby.' We do need to be proactive to keep our system dialed into health these days, so I suggest that you do some experimenting and find some practices and food habits that work for your life and that you find enjoyable. Developing momentum in the right direction is the best health insurance policy, and it's not that expensive. Often times we think that we can't afford health. With the most common cancers costing so much and the toll this kind of disease process takes on the quality of life, taking positive action to be proactive is a well-spent investment. It's not just cancer; heart disease and diabetes are taking huge tolls on people's lives, so it's never too late to get going on course-correcting one's lifestyle. It's easy to feel overwhelmed these days, so it behooves us to focus more on where we already have resources internally and to bring more supply, such as the breath, to our daily lives for greater health and enjoyment in the moment.

The Water That Flows

The mostly water-based system within us that is our lymph, is an invisible mystery to most. Yet it is a key foundation of our health. Becoming more knowledgeable and aligned with our lymph is a way to open our lives up to become more fluid in a variety of ways, some directly helping our biological system, some more on the emotional and mental levels. If we are born 70-75% water, then we most surely must be meant to embody fluidity in the way that we live.

The old adage "running water clears itself" is also modern wisdom. Just as inner circulation of fluids aids the lymph system to do its work, learning to recognize and go with the flow of positivity in life naturally creates more happiness psychologically that also registers on the physical level as a form of ease. Positive emotional states are good for lymph system function so it is time to make the lymph and our emotional flow a priority in life.

Having read this book, I leave you with this request—to play and discover more fluidity in your life in a variety of ways, making it a part of expanding enjoyment and new discoveries. In recognizing our lymph as a great river of life and its vital role to both cleanse and renew, may we commit to this simple message in our lives: to let go when it is time and allow the good to be received as we become more flowing within and without.

[5]

Summing It Up

Top Take-Aways to Optimize Lymph Function

- Hydrate with water and plants with high water content.

- Take time to breathe full, easy breaths each day.

- Eat primarily fresh, whole food and increase your body's intake of nutrients through good food choices, while decreasing your toxic intake. Learn ways to keep cutting back on processed food as part of your lifestyle.

- Move more, and be sedentary less. Movement stimulates proper function of the lymph system. Because the lymph has a vast role in microcirculation to keep us clear, we need to get moving to support our lymph function. The lymph is primarily moved by muscle contractions in the body (activity = muscle contractions) and the breath, so increase these two functions to keep the lymph flowing as it is designed. Make it as fun as possible (fun = likely to be repeated).

- Take enzymes and eat more living food (raw) with their enzymes intact to increase absorption and clear debris from the body.

Toward Greater Lymph Flow

- Drink cran-water because its fruit acids will work to emulsify fats transported through lymph fluid, break down cellular debris and flush the lymph.

- Drink lemon water in the morning and/or during the day to alkalize body fluids and boost lymph function as well as calm the mind and counter stress.

- Drink juices and smoothies as part of the daily diet to help hydrate and alkalize the body. Ingesting nutrient dense plant-infused drinks is an easy way to alkalize the body, and decrease tightness and constriction of tissues, including the lymph vessels.

- Use enzymes, herbs, spices and supplements to help to breakdown proteins and fats and decongest the lymph tissues and fluids.

- Rebound, do stretches, yoga and walking as simple ways to support natural movement in the fluids.

- Dry brush the skin to increase lymph circulation and clearing.

- Find ways to improve your lymph system function while relaxing, like with mudras, breathing practices and acupressure discs.

- Make eating well a healthy hobby and way to enjoy life. Plants are generally alkalizing, so add them in as much as possible to balance the many ways that modern life is acidifying. Experiment with protocols and food habits that work best to increase vitality. It's a great way to make use of your creative energy for positive and pleasant benefits. Our health is our greatest wealth to enjoy for sure.

- Make hydration a way of life—it's that important. Experiment with drinking water when you have a pull to eat something within a few hours of having a meal. While I believe in eating small meals often for my own regimen and know it works, often we are eating as a somewhat confused response to a body signal for water. Over time, we can help our body to function better by replenishing the body's supply of water regularly.

    As Drs. Murad and Cousens have indicated, eating more hydrating food with structured water in it is also a straightforward way to increase the volume and quality of water within that is key to the body's ability to cleanse and renew itself.

- Make self-nurturing a way of life, because it is key to living long and well.

- Find ways to move out of your head and into your heart to increase your enjoyment of life and support the easy flow of fluids (not constricted by stress). Learn to shift gears. Find ways to lessen stress and improve adaptation and resilience (play, laugh, imagine and create, do yoga, tai chi, qigong, meditation, chanting, prayer). Your life is worth it! We can take it for granted that life will bring challenges, and we need to build in rejuvenating tools and practices that balance stress and the toll of daily life.

- Find a professional practitioner to help boost lymph function and experience a higher calibration of health as well as increased flow in life.

Some of the Best Ingestibles for Lymph Function

Below is a recap of some of the best ingestibles mentioned in this book to support the lymph in its wide-ranging role in the body.

- Hydrate With Fruits and Veggies Plant sources of pure living structured water are good for the lymph system as well as the whole body. Plants that have a lot of water supply the body with the best hydration possible, so eat more raw living food. Some good sources: pomegranate, dark-colored fruits (especially berries), watermelon, cantaloupe, pineapple, pears, grapes, bananas, carrots, celery, tomatoes, cabbage, radishes, zucchini, bell peppers, spinach, green peas, eggplant, broccoli and cauliflower.

- Cram in the Cranberries This is a very effective source of fruit acids and enzymes that can break down fat so that the body can keep it moving and absorb it for good use. Because the fats are so important, the work of cranberries to assist in digestion and lymph movement is quite a contribution to healthy function.

- Cool It With Citrus Lemons are especially good. A very hydrating and cooling form of fruit, citrus also helps cleanse, so it supports the work of the lymph. This is a top-pick fruit source of potent purifying enzymes and antioxidant plant compounds that are very beneficial for the body. Add lemon to water in the morning, either at room temperature or hot, to boost your detox at the beginning of the day.

- Eat Beautiful Beets This brightly colored root really can't be beat for enhancing lymph function. It helps to scrub the intestines where most of the lymph is (the GALT) so the villi function well. One of nature's best cleansing vegetables, beets contain antioxidants known as betalains, and they are very effective to get the lymph moving.

- Get Your Reds Both manjistha, the Indian root highly revered in Ayurveda for its ability to counter lymph stagnation, and the commonly known American Ceanothus plant known as red root, are premier lymph movers. Add to this list red clover for its lymph-moving mojo.

- Mineralize With Iodine This mineral is vital for its role as a lymph mover and detox catalyst, not to mention its support of the thyroid gland, so important to proper metabolism in the body. Iodine is also considered to be a protective element against cancer. Sea veggies and unrefined sea salt are wonderful sources. Other good sources of this important trace mineral: cranberries! Some beans with good offerings of iodine include pinto, navy and kidney beans. Strawberries and potato skins are two other very delectable options to increase one's iodine level.

- Eat Powerful Flavonoid Foods **Brightly-hued fruits and vegetables provide powerhouse compounds to enhance the body's antioxidant ability. Oxidation is a natural outworking of metabolism, so even without other toxin intake, we need these forms of food to counter the debris that is a result of the body's basic work. Apples are one of the most popular with quercetin, and the South African tea known as rooibos is a good source as well. Another source of popular flavonoids known as catechins come from green tea.**

- Get Your Greens **Many different types of greens are available to help the body to cleanse itself. Chlorophyll is good for the blood and it is a precursor of lymph fluid, so it is a nutrient that builds the body fluids. Both leafy greens and micro greens (the young growth that develops right after the sprout phase) are loaded with nutrients. Include them in your food choices to improve your blood and calm your nervous system. Parsley, basil, oregano, cilantro and other green herbs can be used to build blood and provide tasty and healthy benefits for the body, including that of green chlorophyll, to cleanse.**

- Spice It Up **Some of the best spices for the lymph include the ever-popular garlic, turmeric, the great Indian spice with widely beneficial effects, and ginger root. They all increase circulation and have other benefits to promote good lymph function.**

- The More Adaptogenic Herbs, the Better **Both echinacea and astragalus are effective anti-inflammatories that support proper lymph node and vessel functioning, helping to keep the lymph from congestion. Echinacea helps the lymphocytes, and both echinacea and turmeric stimulate macrophages to function better. Macrophages are the recyclers of waste and foreign invaders (viruses and other opportunistic organisms), so increasing them is great for immune function.**

- **Don't Forget the Healthy Veggies of the Sea** Ocean-sourced plants and algae are high in the minerals needed for proper alkalizing. They are perfect support for the lymph system to balance the body's fluids and clear out excess water where it has built up. They also provide a boost to support the waste-clearing function of the lymph with their natural ability to detox heavy metals and other toxins. Include wonderful blue-green spirulina, forest green chlorella and seaweed ribbons in the form of dulse, wakame, kelp, hiziki, kombu, Irish moss, bladderwrack, nori and arame in your diet to harvest the benefits these jewels of the sea offer. Remember, experimenting with taste is a good thing for finding healthy options. (See Resources for a kelp-infused chickpea salad.)

- **Make It a Priority to Eat Healthy Fats** The body needs healthy fats for brain function and to keep cell membranes vital. As a transporter of fats, the quality of fats needs to be considered so as not to overburden the lymph system with fat that is indigestible and a contributor to clogged lymph. Omega-3s are needed in much greater supply than omega-6s, but the standard diet is full of the omega-6 forms of fat. Some of the best omega-3s are found in wild salmon, chia and flax. Other healthy fats are found in avocados and walnuts. The body can easily recognize nature's fats, unlike many of the common, highly processed fats that the body registers as foreign and has to struggle to metabolize.

- **Scrubbers Are Very Helpful** Eat good fiber in the form of veggies and fruits. For example, beets and okra are good intestinal scrubbers. These wonderful plants can keep those tiny villi upright and doing their vital work. Apples, with their ample pectin and malic acid, are also good at clearing toxins. You can also add fiber by using psyllium and ground flax. The scrubbers help metabolic waste and toxins to make their exit in a timely manner.

Making Lifestyle Changes

The best practice? One that you'll do, most of the time.

Give yourself permission to experiment and find out what works by trying something out for a period of time. See how you feel, whether your perspective shifts and what you learn about yourself. A key practice of becoming more effective in life is to accept that we're always in the process of discovery. Through living, we're engaging with our own creative life energy and there's learning in everything that we do. Be curious about what's going on in life, both things that feel expansive and those that are stressful or challenging. Open to a bigger way of seeing what is presenting itself in your world.

Amusement with oneself and our foibles is key. Yes, that's easier said than done, but it's really helpful. Everyone forgets, falls down and has to find forgiveness and resolve to start again. Let yourself be human while striving for something that will show more of who you really are. This is the core of living as a creative being.

Go for the gold with all the gusto you can muster and remember that everyone needs a support team, whether in their heads or in their life (or both!). Engage with others who will sincerely urge you on, celebrate your wins and be constructive and encouraging when you have to start over. Here are some steps to recall:

- Make a choice of one thing that feels right as a challenge of change at this time.

- Set your intent and begin to alter your life to fit in some new lifestyle choice. Make it a learning adventure, like traveling to a new place. It is. You're journeying to a new, more expanded consciousness by making any kind of shift.

- Allow that it will feel different and maybe not much fun sometimes, but do your best to focus on the discovery that it brings—of new understanding about yourself in the process of change and what it is like to learn new things, make choices, take risks, value yourself more deeply and move forward.

- Keep some notes about what you notice. It can often be quite informative in gaining new awareness and remembering how you've taken action to engage in life.

- When you don't meet your goals all the time, just let yourself begin again. We all have the opportunity to wake up and begin anew each day. Some days are easier than others, and change is a practice like any creative form. It takes discipline and applied will to become good at anything we set our mind to do. Remember that the qualities of play, experimentation and discovery are worthwhile aspects of anything we're engaged in, and allow many openings of awareness.

- Keep in mind that each life course-correction has bigger long-term effects for the better than we can see in the daily round. Looking back a month or a year later, we'll be glad that we were proactive. Taking action builds confidence and courage to take on bigger challenges with enjoyable and fulfilling rewards.

My Favorite Take-away

Choose one thing to experiment with and if it feels right, make it a practice, part of your lifestyle. Then add in something else that feels right. Course correcting simply over time is very beneficial and not overly complicated, i.e., you can do it!

Remember, These Are Ways We Hinder Lymph System Function

- Lack of internal water, i.e., dehydration
- Poor diet with lots of acidic food and drinks, and too few alkaline drinks, foods and minerals

- Unresolved stress and few mind-body practices to resolve stress and increase adaptation in life
- Shallow breathing, only breathing through the top of the lungs
- Sedentary ways of living, little body activity
- Poor posture, restricting internal lymph flow and function
- Lack of sleep that reduces the body's time to detox and renew itself overnight
- Little time spent outdoors, tuning to nature's cycles
- Living with little heart happiness

Printed in Great Britain
by Amazon